Endorsement

Art gives us a language where our own words are not enough. Bottomless sorrow, trembling happiness, anxiety, love, regret, and hope.

Kristine T. G. Hardeberg's book, *Art History for Everyone,* is a straightforward, simple, and easy-to-read introduction to the history of art before 1900. In other words, the basis for the art of our time. Although this book is for beginners, I also learned new things, having studied the subject for 50 years.

Hardeberg writes with enthusiasm, joy, and curiosity, making this a book most people will enjoy reading.

"You use a mirror to see your face, but you use art to see your soul," said writer George Bernard Shaw. Art reminds us of who we are and who we want to be.

Morten Krogvold
Writer/Celebrity Photographer

Art History for Everyone

LEARN ABOUT ART IN A FUN, EASY, NO-NONSENSE WAY

**To Kristine Stangeland,
who saw this book before it existed.**

Published by Ethos Collective™
PO Box 43, Powell, OH 43065
www.ethoscollective.vip

Library of Congress Cataloging:

LCCN: 2023907452
Paperback: 978-1-63680-163-6
Hardcover: 978-1-63680-164-3
Ebook: 978-1-63680-165-0

Available in hardcover, softcover, and e-book.

To protect the privacy of those who have shared their stories with the author, some details and names have been changed. Any Internet addresses (websites, blogs, etc.) and telephone numbers printed in this book are offered as a resource. They are not intended in any way to be or imply an endorsement by Ethos Collective, nor does Ethos Collective vouch for the content of these sites and numbers for the life of this book.

This information in this book is not intended to be a substitute for the medical advice or treatment of a licensed physician or other licensed healthcare provider nor does it constitute medical advice. You should consult with your doctor or other trusted medical professional about any matters relating to your health or any symptoms or ailments that may require medical intervention. You are encouraged to consult with your physician or other licensed healthcare provider before starting or stopping any medication or before implementing any treatment or therapy discussed in this book. Although the author and publisher have made every effort to ensure that the information in this book was correct at press time, the author and publisher do not assume and hereby disclaim any liability to any party for any loss, damage, or disruption caused by errors or omissions, whether such errors or omissions result from negligence, accident, or any other cause.

The information contained in this book is for information and entertainment purposes only. This publication is designed to provide competent and reliable information regarding the subject matter covered. However, it is sold with the understanding that the author and publisher are not engaged in rendering legal, financial, or other professional advice. Laws and practices often vary from state to state, and if legal or other expert assistance is required, the services of a professional should be sought. Although the author and publisher have made every effort to ensure that the information in this book was correct at time of release, the author and publisher do not assume and hereby disclaim any liability to any party for any loss, damage, or disruption caused by errors or omissions, whether such errors or omissions result from negligence, accident, or any other cause.

Art History for Everyone

LEARN ABOUT ART IN A FUN, EASY, NO-NONSENSE WAY

Kristine T. G. Hardeberg

ethos
collective

Contents

Read this first!

I'm so happy you chose to open this book. You're about to join me on an exciting discovery trip into the world of art, and this journey will enrich your life.

For more than ten years, I've been teaching art history. Online, in classrooms, and on tours in different countries. Often, I hear people excuse themselves for knowing too little about art. Or they dismiss the subject as too complicated and too overwhelming, saying, "Help, I don't understand!" Or they may think it's irrelevant, "This isn't for me."

Art history seems foreign to many people. When individuals hear colleagues, friends, or family members talk about this or that piece of art, they have no idea what to say or how to respond.

This is natural—when we lack knowledge about something, it does seem incomprehensible and strange, as well as difficult or just plain boring.

I've written this book to show you that art history doesn't need to be foreign and difficult; rather, it is both fun and exciting! And that it concerns all of us.

My students tell me that they are surprised at how interesting and fun it is to learn about art. Some say, "My everyday life suddenly is more colorful," and others tell me, "My life is changed!"

This is how it is. When we learn something, and it doesn't need to be a lot, we open a door to a whole new world.

The history of art is full of beautiful experiences, surprises, and aha moments. Suddenly, you see the references in the lyrics of a song you love or understand what that movie scene was all about. And even more fun: Suddenly, you realize that you know a whole lot more about art than you thought you did.

What if you, too, could crawl over this invisible fence, and become excited about art?

This book opens art history for you, teaches you important words and expressions, and gives you the tools you need to enjoy art on your own.

And you can look forward to visiting art galleries and museums, at home or in other cities.

Quick note: When I was seventeen, I visited a great museum, the Louvre, in Paris. It didn't turn out the way I had hoped. You see, I had never heard about the restaurant method. I'll talk more about that later, so you can enjoy those museum visits.

This book focuses on Western European art history, from classical Antiquity through modern days, with an emphasis on the centuries between 1400 and 1900. I've had some difficult choices to make. As you can imagine, the topic of art history is vast. Instead of covering everything, I've chosen a few periods and some important artists which I believe will give you a good overview.

This book is for those who don't know anything about art history. But it's also for those who already know a little or a lot.

You see, art meets us exactly where we are in life. You don't need a university degree to find art interesting. The proof? Look at the children. They're amazing role models when it comes to appreciating art. They approach art without prejudice and without thinking that they don't know enough. They simply head in, ask questions, and wonder.

Somewhere deep inside, we're all children. We carry with us this curious child who longs to learn, understand, and figure out how and why.

I'll be your tour guide as you discover the world of art. Let's get going!

CHAPTER 1

How Do You Look at Art?

You *are* good enough

Your friends want to visit the museum, but you hesitate. "Go ahead. I'll wait for you here at the café," you say and smile while grimacing on the inside. Maybe part of you wanted to go in, but you don't know if you can take it. You feel there is so much you don't understand, and the others seem to know it all.

The thing is, we often make a gallery visit a lot more complicated than it needs to be. We observe other people in museums and galleries, and it looks as if they're following a set of mysterious rules about how people should behave in front of a painting or a sculpture. They tilt their head, cross their arms, and nod slowly with a knowing expression. "What do they see that I don't?" you think.

Theodor Kittelsen: Far, far away
Soria Moria Palace shimmered
like gold, 1900. National
Museum, Oslo, Norway

12

Good news: We don't have to nod or cross our arms. We don't need to do anything special at all. I'll tell you a secret: The others don't know everything either.

Meet the art as the person you are, exactly where you are in life, with your experiences, joys, sorrows, ideas, and associations. There is even a big chance that you'll see something that the so-called experts have never noticed!

Be an explorer

We should all be explorers when we approach art. Be like those who ventured beyond, through unknown landscapes without a map. They carried nothing except the wish to get ahead, learn something new, and hope for good experiences at the journey's end.

Don't you have a clue as to what to look for in a painting? Have you never heard about this or that artist? It's completely okay! If you give that piece of art a chance, just like the explorer who sets out into unknown territory through the fog and hidden valleys, you may arrive at a beautiful place where you want to stay for a long time.

Make space for curiosity. It is necessary!

Be childlike

Said in another way, we must be like children! Because they are the real explorers. They set out on this journey we call life without knowledge or navigation systems, and, even more importantly— without prejudice. Everything is exciting to them. "Look, a cat!" they squeal happily. A stick on the ground or a few pebbles may be admired for minutes. Wonder is a natural part of every moment of their day.

And we were there once, all of us. We had an ingenuous outlook on the world until we grew up and forgot how exciting life really is. We got stuck in already-defined attitudes. Limitations ended the joy.

Many adults prefer already knowing what they learn. Or, said in another way, they like the feeling of having confirmed what they think they know already.

Children are not like that. They are attracted to the unknown, the undiscovered, anything that pushes the limits. They lean towards the mysteries and the magic. They are curious, they want to understand, and they ask questions. And that is why they learn so fast.

If we—at least now and then—try to come back to this way of experiencing life, and if we try to see art in a childlike way, a whole new world will open in front of us.

Maybe you see a work of art, and initially, you understand absolutely nothing. But remember that you are more than good enough. Remember that what you carry with you, your experiences and emotions, thoughts, and ideas, count just as much as anybody else's! Be open to what may happen when you sit in front of a painting or a sculpture, maybe see something new, or think something that never before crossed your mind. That's how you open the door for art to be exciting.

The questions are more important than the answers. Don't be afraid of what you don't understand or don't think you understand.

The next time you are in front of an artwork, either in a gallery or on the internet: Take your time. Have an open mind. Let that painting or sculpture talk to you. What do you see? What do you feel? What do you experience?

The Restaurant Method

To have the outlook of an explorer is one of the keys to having a good experience with art. But there is another, equally important key: Don't bite off too much.

I was seventeen years old the first time I visited the beautiful Louvre Museum in Paris. I was excited about the trip and had been looking forward to it, but the experience didn't turn out the way I'd expected.

After waiting in line for what seemed like forever, I followed the crowds through endless hallways, up long stairways, and through room after room filled with images and sculptures. Where were we heading? To the *Mona Lisa,* of course.

Finally, we arrived. I spotted the painting in between all the people who were crowded there. It was smaller than I expected, but still, there it was, the famous portrait by Leonardo da Vinci.

But then, I felt so disappointed that I almost broke down in tears.

I wasn't disappointed with the Louvre or the painting. No, I was disappointed

The role of the artist is to ask *the questions. Not answer them.*

—Anton Chekhov

with myself. I knew this was supposed to be a great moment, but I couldn't feel it. All I felt was tired. In fact, I was exhausted.

There were paintings and statues everywhere I looked, so many that I long ago had lost track of what I had seen. All that beautiful art made my head swirl, and I had no idea where to look or why.

In the end, I stood in the middle of the room, feeling completely lost. Most of all, I wanted to leave, but I couldn't. I was in the Louvre! I felt I should try to see as much as possible.

My eyes swept up and down huge walls filled with artwork. My feet hurt, but the halls continued forever.

Finally, I couldn't take it anymore, and I left the museum, very disappointed with myself.

Today, I know what I did wrong, and I want you to take notice here because this is maybe the most important point you will learn from this book. You see, as a seventeen-year-old, I had never heard of *the Restaurant Method*. It is something my older self would define.

The Restaurant Method is all about treating a museum as if it were a dining establishment.

When you are in a big museum, like the Louvre, the Metropolitan Museum of Art, or the National Gallery of Art, you must make choices. You will select a few pieces of art, or at least stick with a few rooms and skip the rest.

"That's impossible!" people tell me. "What if this is my only time at the Louvre! I should, at least, try to see as much as possible. If not, I will regret it later."

No, you shouldn't.

You must think about a large museum or gallery as if it were a restaurant. Yes, a restaurant!

Picture yourself with the once-in-a-lifetime experience of eating at a world-famous restaurant. It's a place you have read about and dreamed of experiencing, and now you are finally there. A waiter comes to the table to take your order. Would you answer, "Give me as much food as possible"?

Is your goal to eat every item on their menu? Drink every wine? If you try this, I can promise that, before long, you will be too full to continue, or you will even become sick. And that restaurant will be a horrible memory.

Of course, you wouldn't approach the dinner in this way. Instead, you learn a little about the menu so that you know the difference between the dishes, or you ask the waiter to help you choose before selecting a few dishes. Most of what they offer, you'll probably never taste. That's life!

After making your selections, you don't rush. You take your time to enjoy the creations placed before you, and after a while, if there is space in your stomach, you'll order dessert. This restaurant experience will likely remain a beautiful memory.

You must think about art galleries exactly like this. Learn a little about art so that you can make your choices or ask for help in the gallery. Choose a few pieces or a few rooms. And then, take your time to enjoy the paintings or sculptures. *Really* see them.

After a while, take a break. Go to the cafeteria and have something to drink or eat lunch. Let your body rest. More importantly, let your mind rest. You see, art makes our heads "full," just as food makes our stomachs full.

And then, and only if you have space in your head, you go back in and see a little bit more. (This would be the dessert.)

Most of what the gallery or museum offers you'll probably never see. That's unavoidable, and it must be like this if you want a good experience that you will keep as a cherished memory for the rest of your life.

But remember what I said about being an explorer or a child because you may have learned about art and made a beautiful plan when your eyes hit something else, a piece of art you've never thought of or heard about before, but which suddenly beckons. When that happens, you should listen to that inner child, the explorer, who leads you to discover something new.

And who knows, maybe this artwork will change your life. Art is powerful, and we'll talk more about this in our next chapter.

CHAPTER 2

Do We Need Art?

Andrej Smolak: "Dove of Peace and Prisoner, 1999. The Berlin Wall (East Side Gallery)

What do you think? Is art only about decoration? Is it something we can manage without? Or, do you think, like me, that art is important yes, even more important than we usually think!

Being Creative

Humans have always expressed themselves through images or shapes, saying something about something without using everyday language. We've been making art since the Stone Age.

The cave paintings in Lascaux, France, are about 15,000 years old.

And you, who read these words right now, are an artist. Whether you know it or not. At least, you have once been one.

You see, we're all born with a strong urge to create, to make an impression on the world. We are creative beings.

Look at the children. Their imagination is vivid, and they're constantly creating something. Their artistry is present before they can talk. Children draw—on paper, floors, walls, and furniture. They make sandcastles and snowmen; they create magical creatures from the soap bubbles in the bathtub. They build, they craft, they use their imagination, and they see no limits as to what can become an image or a sculpture.

Picasso said, "Every child is an artist. The problem is to remain an artist once he grows up."

Every child is an artist. The problem is to remain an artist once he grows up.

—Pablo Picasso

Of course, we shouldn't all be full-time artists, the world would be a strange place, and we would go hungry and cold, but we all carry with us that child we used to be, that creative urge we all have in us.

What did you love making when you were a child? Did you draw? Paint? Build?

How about giving your creativity space once in a while? Blow life into that little spark you carry inside. You don't have to show your art to anybody—it can be for your eyes only—and of course, it doesn't have to be visual art. It can be something else, like music. Do you sing or play an instrument? Dance? Maybe your art is about crafts, like knitting, sewing, woodworking, or cooking. There are a thousand ways to express yourself creatively, and no matter what it is for you, we all benefit from doing something creative once in a while. It's not a meaningless pastime; on the contrary, it enhances your day, and often, it clears your thoughts and helps solve life's challenges. Suddenly, you experience that "Yes! Now, I know!" feeling.

Looking around us, we see examples of human creativity everywhere: maybe a beautiful building or colorful flowerbeds in a park or by someone's driveway. And, of course, statues and street art, although we tend to overlook these examples because we have seen them so many times.

To Experience Art

More than anything, we need to experience art.

Every day one should at least hear one little song read one good poem, see one fine painting and—if at all possible—speak a few sensible words.

—Johann Wolfgang von Goethe

Art gives us a language for all we don't have words for. Art can comfort us, and I'll return to that in a minute when I show you a very special work of art.

Have your eyes filled with tears when you heard a piece of music that is not sad? It may also happen when you see a painting or while watching a film. Suddenly you're crying, without anything being sad in that music, that image, or that film.

Sometimes you know why. Maybe that painting reminded you of baking cookies with Grandma, who has passed away. Or, that song reminded you of a fun date in a relationship that ended. But, then again, there may be times when you can think of no logical reason for crying. What on earth is that about?

You use a glass mirror to see your face. But you use works of art to see your soul.

—George Bernhard Shaw

I believe that art gives us a language for all that we can't explain. Art speaks to something other than our intellect and shouldn't necessarily be understood rationally. Art hits us in our hearts, and it may trigger emotions like love, hate, happiness, grief, jealousy, humor, irritation, hope, and regret—all these things that make us human, and maybe remind us that we have a soul.

The Stendhal Syndrome

Art even has the power to knock us over. The French author Stendhal (19th century) describes how he felt unwell after a visit to Florence, Italy, where he was surrounded by great art. His heart was beating way too fast, and he felt dizzy and almost fainted. The beauty was too much for him. Every year in Florence, there are examples of what now is known as the Stendhal syndrome. At the hospital in the middle of the city, they treat tourists suffering from palpitations, symptoms presenting as panic attacks, and even hallucinations.

CHAPTER 3

Periods and Trends in Art History

Many of us have tried to read the label next to a painting but given up because the text is full of words that make no sense to us.

When we dive into art history, sooner or later, we will come across its professional language and expressions we don't understand. I prefer talking about art using everyday language, but you may find it handy to know a few technical terms. I'm thinking about the periods and "isms" we'll come across.

If we learn at least a few of these words, art and art history will be a whole lot easier to follow and learn. Picture a closet or storage space with no shelves where everything is piled up. If you put in some shelves, you can sort everything: pants go here, shirts go there, and so on. At a glance, you'll have an overview of what's stored in that closet.

The periods in art history are such shelves. The shelves help us sort the knowledge and the different artists we learn about. Such categories make art history easier to learn and, especially, remember what we learned.

So that our closet doesn't become too full, we'll not go into detail about all the periods and trends there are. Instead, I have picked out a few, the ones I believe will give you a good journey and a good overview of the history of art.

Let's start by going far, back to ancient Greece and Rome.

The Parthenon Temple, Athens

Venus of Milo, 130-100 BC.
The Louvre, Paris

Antiquity

Picture this: You are standing in one of Athens's streets, looking up at the Acropolis Hill. The temple ruins, several thousand years old, talk to us about those glory days we call classical antiquity. This period was roughly two thousand years ago, plus or minus a few hundred years.

The Greek civilization and then the Roman represented, respectively, the best of Western culture in art, architecture, science, and philosophy. They had exact standards concerning beauty and realism in art, and they kept these standards while building temples, palaces, theaters, and sports arenas. Important architectural elements included columns, archways, and domes. Some of their artists wrote and philosophized, while others painted, made mosaics, or sculpted in marble and bronze.

Statue of Emperor Augustus, 1ˢᵗ century.
The Vatican Museums

Duccio:
Madonna and Child, 1283–1284.
Museo dell'Opera Metropolitana del Duomo, Siena

Medieval Era

With the fall of the Roman Empire around the year 400 AD, Europe entered a dangerous time. For almost a thousand years, the European continent was marked by unrest and conquests. Power-hungry princes and warlords fought over land and people. War wasn't the exception but the norm, and large populations were constantly on the move, fleeing war, violence, and abuse. The effects of war were, like today, poverty, disease, and death. The people of Europe experienced much misery, fear, and uncertainty.

Other things that suffered during this time were art and science because it's not when your life is in danger that you paint pictures or think deep thoughts. We could say that art and science went into hiding in monasteries. Thanks to monks and nuns, art was still created. In the monasteries, books were written, pictures were painted, and sculptures were carved.

But art and science need impulses and a dialog to evolve, and art changed remarkably little during these one thousand years. Medieval artists didn't focus on realism, so, to us, their paintings may seem artificial or stylized.

Madonna and Child

The Virgin Mary and Baby Jesus, often called *Madonna and Child*, is without comparison the most common theme in all of Western Art history. Why? Because for several hundred years, the church was the main employer for artists in Europe. There was a never-ending demand for altarpieces in churches, chapels, and private homes.

Through a big part of the medieval era, there were strict rules about how to paint this theme. Mary looks pious, wearing a simple dress and a cloak covering her hair. The child seems like an adult in miniature, a strange doll sitting on her arm. There were no expectations for art to be realistic or to have a three-dimensionality. It was as if the knowledge from antiquity was utterly forgotten.

And for a thousand years, artists depicted *Madonna and Child* in more or less the same way. But then came the next period, the Renaissance, and everything changed.

CHAPTER 4

Renaissance

The Renaissance is when Europe once again bloomed, and Florence, a small city in Tuscany, would become home to what we now know as the biggest art movement in history.

Around the year 1400, Europe had become more orderly, with functioning city-states and some democracy. People could settle down and build houses, churches, and palaces. Once again, they could give space to ideas and ambition. And where did they find inspiration? They looked back to classical Rome in that glorious time before the "dark ages".

The word *Renaissance* is of French origin and means re-birth. What was born again during this time was classical antiquity, its thoughts, ideas, and ways of doing things.

People living during the Renaissance invented the term *medieval era* (Middle Ages) to describe those thousand years that separated them from antiquity.

Now, we could see countless innovations within science, architecture, and art, resulting in a standard for Western culture to last for centuries to come.

It's time to meet some of the artists from the Renaissance.

Jan van Eyck
1380 or 1390–1441

Let's go to the city of Bruges, in today's Belgium. A merchant named Arnolfini lived there in the fifteenth century. When he was about to become engaged to be married, he wanted to immortalize it all in a painting, and he gave the commission to the painter Jan van Eyck.

Despite being quite small and perhaps seeming insignificant at first glance, the Arnolfini portrait is full of symbolism, and it is considered one of the most important paintings of the early Renaissance. Van Eyck probably made a pilgrimage to Florence, where he learned from the masters. Then he traveled back home to Flanders and impressed everybody with his new art.

In this painting, we can see Giovanni de Nicolao Arnolfini with his beloved as they make their solemn vows. Van

Jan van Eyck: *The Arnolfini Portrait*,
about 1434. National Gallery, London

Eyck could have made this a lot easier to paint by placing them in front of a wall. Instead, he has chosen to place them in an interior, where the lines slope inward into the picture—perhaps to show that he was one of the first to learn the new art of painting according to the rules of central perspective (learn more about this in Perspective in Drawing and Painting, p. 30). If you follow the lines in the floor, ceiling, window, or bed, you will find what we call the vanishing point. Right at that point, we see a mirror on the wall. In this mirror, you can see the couple from behind, the painter, dressed in blue, and behind him, you can see yet another person. We don't know who it is, but he or she is placed there in the mirror to assure us that there were two witnesses present, which was necessary for the betrothal to be valid.

This new realism is typical of Renaissance art. Artists wanted images to reflect reality. Notice how masterfully Van Eyck shows us the different surfaces: the brass of the chandelier, the wooden floor, the fur trim on Arnolfini's coat, and the little dog, who almost seems to be jumping out of the picture. Van Eyck is also one of the first to use a new invention—oil painting. Until then, artists usually mixed pigment powder with eggs to make paint, which was called tempera, but by using oil as a binder, new possibilities opened up. Oil dries more slowly than eggs, making it much easier to paint what you want, change the colors, or blend them gradually.

Can you spot the artist's signature? At the time, artists weren't supposed to sign their work, yet several found ways to put their names on paintings or sculptures. Take a look at the wall in the back of the room. It's written in Latin: "Jan van Eyck was here".

Symbols

Because few people at the time knew how to read, symbols were a lot more important than we may understand fully today. Let's look at a few of the symbols hidden in this painting.

Have you seen the fruit on the windowsill? Perhaps Arnolfini wanted to brag, to hint about the fact that they were rich and could afford oranges, a fruit considered a luxury at the time. But that fruit may as well be about something else entirely: a wish for a fruitful marriage.

Notice, also, the bed behind them. It covers a large part of the painting, and it is draped in red, symbolizing passion and love.

As you admire the masterly painted brass chandelier, you may notice only one burning candle. That single candle is a symbol of God's presence. An engagement at the time was considered part of the wedding, thus a sacred act.

The couple is not wearing shoes. You can see sandals in the foreground and some more in the back of the painting. I doubt that people had a habit of taking off their shoes indoors. Being shoeless tells us once again that something important, something sacred, is occurring. To take off one's shoes is considered a symbolic act in many religions. "Take off your sandals, for the place where you are standing is holy ground," it says in the Bible (Acts 7:33, ESV).

The little dog was perhaps not there, but the artist may have added it because dogs, in art history, represent loyalty and fidelity.

Now that we have learned a little about Renaissance art, it's time for us to go to the city where it was born. Let's head to Florence!

Florence

It is the beginning of the fifteenth century. We can hear hammer blows from multiple construction sites around us. Palaces, churches, and statues are being built all over the city. We hear the buzz of voices in Italian, Greek, and many other languages. The Renaissance is happening, and it is here in Florence that it all began! Yes, this beautiful little town in Tuscany quickly became the most important city in the Western world, and it would retain that reputation for several hundred years.

Florence's historic center has changed very little in five hundred years. Strolling through the narrow, cobbled streets today, you see much of Florence as it looked during the Renaissance.

Imagine if we could go back in time and experience the tremendous development in art and architecture, as well as in sciences, such as mathematics and astronomy, not to mention the general view on humanity. Human value and dignity, as ethical ideals, took root in the minds of ordinary people and were also reflected in politics.

Everybody traveled to Florence: painters, sculptors, philosophers, architects, writers, astronomers, and mathematicians. They pondered, discussed, and launched big, new ideas, such as the earth orbiting

Florence, the Renaissance city.

The Innocenti Orphanage in Florence
(Spedale degli Innocenti)

the sun and that humans should be able to fly.

Later, these ideas spread throughout Europe, and a great deal of our Western culture to this day originates from Renaissance Florence.

The Innocenti Orphanage

At about this same time in Florence, an unheard-of idea was to build an orphanage. No one had ever thought of such a thing. Orphans had no value—they were unwanted.

Before this, churches and monasteries had cared for orphans, but this new project was to become Europe's first secular orphanage. The community took responsibility for the unfortunate little ones of Florence, and the orphanage was named The Hospital of the Innocents.

The building of the Innocenti orphanage was financed through the powerful Silk Guild in Florence, and they hired Filippo Brunelleschi as the architect. Brunelleschi was a celebrity at the time. He was a typical Renaissance man, having mastered many different art forms.

Brunelleschi was a goldsmith, architect, sculptor, draftsman, engineer, and inventor. He discovered a mathematical method for making a central perspective in painting. He also constructed the great dome of Florence's cathedral, and he built the machinery needed to erect the enormous structure.

Brunelleschi traveled to Rome and made sketches of ruins, archways, columns, and domes, and then he returned to Florence and drew the orphanage, inspired by Rome as it was in classical antiquity.

When you enter the Piazza della Santissima Annunziata from the northwest, you can easily spot the façade of the Innocenti Orphanage, which is considered the world's first Renaissance building. With its clean lines, columns, archways, and its symmetry, the orphanage became the blueprint for what we today know as Renaissance architecture.

Perspective in Drawing and Painting

If we study ancient wall paintings, we realize that in antiquity, people knew how to use perspective in art. They were able to make the illusion of three dimensions on a flat wall. In the medieval era, artists seem to have forgotten these skills because paintings and drawings look flat and unrealistic.

Also, during the Renaissance, Brunelleschi found a way to construct a central perspective mathematically, which would be one of the biggest changes in art. Central perspective is about having all lines meet up in one single point in the middle of the image. This is what we call the vanishing point. We experience the same effect when we see a road or train tracks meet at a point on the horizon.

The Medici Family

Why did this artistic and scientific revolution happen in Florence, a small and "unimportant" town far from Rome?

There are several reasons for this, and one of them is the Medici family.

The Medici were powerful and important to Florence's evolution. They started one of the world's first banks, one that also became the preferred bank of the Pope. Their bank helped money flow through the city. The Medici ruled Florence for centuries, first through their status and financial position and eventually as Grand Dukes, where the title was inherited.

We can thank this family for many of the palaces and churches we see today in Florence. The Medici would also constantly commission new paintings and sculptures, arrange for the translation of ancient texts, and support science and research. We could give them much of the credit for the Renaissance being born in Florence.

In the eighteenth century, the Medici family's office building was converted into an art gallery, and today, the Uffizi Gallery is one of the world's largest and most visited museums.

The Uffizi Gallery is a special building that originally contained the offices of the Medici family. The word *uffizi* means *offices* in Italian.

The Uffizi Gallery in Florence.

Fra Filippo Lippi: *Madonna and Child with Two Angels*, ca. 1465. Uffizi Gallery, Firenze

Fra Filippo Lippi
1406-1469

On the upper floor of the gallery, we find this gem of a painting. I usually call it *The Smiling Angel*.

Do you remember us talking about the paintings of Mary and baby Jesus from the Middle Ages? For a thousand years, this theme was painted more or less the same way, but now, with the revolution of the Renaissance, the style changed.

Now, we can see the perspective. The image is not flat, and we don't feel as if the characters are about to slide off the canvas.

Also, notice the realism. Mary has become a real human being, a contemporary woman from Florence, dressed in the fashion of the time so that the viewers may now relate to her better. She's seated on a chair with a pillow on the armrest, and the artist has painted in a frame within the picture. Perhaps it's just to show off, tell us that he has learned central perspective? Or perhaps it's because he wants us to understand that Mary belongs to two worlds? She is both a human being *and* Queen of Heaven. She combines two realities.

The painting is usually called *Madonna and Child with Two Angels*, but we should keep in mind that the artist himself didn't give this painting a name. Giving titles to artworks is a modern practice. When this image was painted, around 1460-65, everybody knew who they were looking at: the Virgin Mary and baby Jesus being lifted up by two angels.

The Colors of Mary

How could they know the woman was Mary? Among other things, because the painter has given us some clear hints. First of all, both Mary and Baby Jesus have halos above their heads. They're faint but visible if you look closely. The halos symbolize the holy and tell us that we are looking at saints. But to be sure that this is the Virgin Mary, we can look at the colors of her clothes. She's wearing a red dress and a blue cape. These are the colors of the Virgin Mary throughout the history of art. Of course, there are exceptions, but in most paintings, she is dressed in these colors. The red dress symbolizes the blood and suffering that will come. After all, she will lose her son in a horrible way! Red also symbolizes the earth because Mary

A Little Gossip

Fra is short for *fratello*, which means brother in Italian. In English, we could as well call him Brother Filippo. He was a monk, but he was not cut out for monastic life—he kept running away from the monastery. Filippo fell in love with an upper-class woman, Lucrezia Buti, and ran away with her. Soon after, she became pregnant. This was a great scandal in Florence, and he could not return to the monastery after this. The lovers were probably whispered and laughed about throughout the city. But everything turned out well for Filippo and Lucrezia. They started a family with several children, and he opened his own artist workshop, where he was very successful. Among his more famous apprentices were Sandro Botticelli and Filippino Lippi, his first-born son. It is possibly little Filippino who is the model for the grinning angel. We think the model for baby Jesus is their second child, a girl named Sandra. And then it is reasonable to think that Lucrezia was the model for Mary.

Models

During the Renaissance, it was customary to paint from living models. Before this, artists usually painted "ideal faces," which often looked alike. Now, however, it became increasingly important to capture authentic facial expressions and realistic movements that could be recognized by those who view the piece.

Botticelli: *Madonna del Magnificat*, c. 1481-83. Uffizi Gallery, Florence

was a human being, like us. Blue symbolizes the sky, and it is also a royal color. Mary is often referred to as the Queen of Heaven.

One angel is barely visible behind the child, while the other completely steals the show, looking directly at us with a triumphant smile as if to say, "Look at me! I get to be in the picture, and I get to hold the child!" I love that angel!

Botticelli
1445–1510

His name was Alessandro di Filipepi, but his first name was shortened to Sandro, and Botticelli was his nickname.

Sandro Botticelli was born in Florence in the middle of the fifteenth century, so he was both a true child of the Renaissance and one of the greatest painters of this era. As a child, he played in the streets around the Ognissanti church. Later, he became one of the apprentices of our friend Fra Filippo Lippi, and before long, Botticelli was a popular painter. The Medici family ensured that he received many commissions, both from the church and the private sector. He even lived in the Medici palace for a while!

Continuing our visit through the Uffizi Gallery, after viewing Fra Filippo's Smiling Angel, we can discover two circular paintings that, at first glance, are quite similar. Such round paintings are called *tondos,* and they were often part of a building's architecture. More specifically, they were attached above doorways in private homes.

The first picture is called *Madonna del Magnificat*. Once again, we see Mary and baby Jesus. Mary is busy writing in a book, and the child helps her, guiding her arm.

In this picture, they are surrounded by not two but five angels. Two of them hold the crown over her head, and the child looks up at the sun, which shines down through it. The sun is a picture of God. A third angel holds the book in which Mary writes, a fourth holds the inkwell, and the fifth sees to it that everything goes well.

What exactly is she writing? The words she is supposed to have said when she

Botticelli: *Madonna Della Melagrana*, c. 1487-90.
Uffizi Gallery, Florence

Botticelli: *The Birth of Venus*, c. 1486. Uffizi Gallery, Florence

was pregnant with Jesus and went to visit her older cousin, Elizabeth. Mary was probably having mixed feelings about the pregnancy, maybe she was scared, but after her cousin welcomed her with open arms and reassured her, she finally felt she could experience her joy. What Mary then said is referred to, in Latin, as the Magnificat: "My soul magnifies the Lord…from now on all generations will call me blessed" (Luke 1:46-48, ESV). This painting is filled with bliss and peace, radiating a warm beauty from Mary's face, the angels, the fabrics, and the crisp colors.

However, have you noticed the fruit in the child's hand? It's a pomegranate, and it's painted into the picture as a hint because it is an important symbol. The red juice of this fruit reminds us of blood, pointing to the passion of Christ, and all the seeds symbolize how something has to "die" in the earth for new life to grow. Thus, the pomegranate becomes a symbol of Christ's suffering, death, and resurrection. In other words, a symbol of the Easter story. If the people of the time did not already understand who this child was, they would understand upon seeing the pomegranate.

If we shift our gaze slightly, we see the second circular painting, which is called *Madonna della melagrana* (*melagrana* is Italian for *pomegranate*). At first glance, the two tondos are similar. In this painting, just like the other one, we see Mary with the child, surrounded by angels. But, where the first painting is filled with warmth and happiness, this one conveys a different mood. Mary looks so sad, as if she is struggling to hold back tears, as if all the sorrow in the world is resting in her gaze. The angels look serious, as if they have deeply understood what will happen

to this child. The pomegranate is included, too, as a focal point.

The angels, who have wings in this picture, but not the first, look both in dress and hairstyle like young men from contemporary Florence. Botticelli may have entered a neighborhood school and asked a few boys to pose as models. In this picture, several of the angels look straight at us as if they are asking us if we know who this child is and what the future has in store for him. The pomegranate gives us the answer.

Why does art have so many symbols?

Symbols in art were extremely important during the Renaissance when most people did not know how to read and write. Symbols were simply understood, something you learned from childhood, the same way you learn to speak and understand gestures and facial expressions. We are surrounded by symbols today, for example, in traffic, in public restrooms, and on maps, but during the Renaissance, they were more prevalent. If we learn about some of these symbols, they open art history to us, making the meaning of those paintings and sculptures a lot more accessible to us modern people. So far in this book, you have already learned about the pomegranate, Mary's colors, the dog, and sandals on the floor, and there are more to come.

With *The Birth of Venus*, we move away from Virgin Mary and Christianity and over to Greek mythology. We have already learned about how people in the Renaissance loved classical antiquity and how they brought back ideas, architecture, and art techniques from ancient Greece and Rome. This also applied to various texts and, among them, stories from classical mythology.

Individuals did not pray to these ancient gods, but they were intrigued by the myths and viewed them as inspiration for art and as stories to learn from. Venus is the goddess of love, and in Greek, her name was Aphrodite.

The Birth of Venus is Botticelli's most famous painting. It was probably ordered as a wedding present for one of the young Medici couples, and several decades after it was painted, art historian Vasari writes that it could be seen in the Villa Castello, one of the summer homes of the Medici family. It is probably the nudity in the painting that is the reason it was not known publicly until a long time after it was painted.

But it is important to realize that this picture does not show a naked woman in a seashell. Absolutely not. What we do see, on the other hand, is Love itself in human shape—Venus being born, that love has come to the world. She comes from the ocean, and standing in a clam, she is blown ashore by the wind gods. This theme originates from a time when everyone believed that the earth was flat and floated on the ocean. The flower goddess Flora is waiting for her on the shore, ready to wrap her in her floral cloak.

What we really are seeing in this painting is that love as a concept comes to the world and becomes part of what is earthly. Not just romantic love but also love for one's friends and family, charity, and goodness. In other words: As creatures of the earth, we receive the ability to love.

Realism, beauty, and harmony are all important concepts of Renaissance art, but

The Birth of Venus, c. 1486.
Uffizi Gallery, Florence. (Detail)

for Botticelli, beauty and harmony were more important than realism. Therefore, he painted Venus's neck to be far too long so that he got exactly that special tilt of the body that fits perfectly to Flora's gown and thus, the harmony he was searching for.

The model for Venus, and for several of Botticelli's Madonnas was Simonetta Vespucci, cousin-in-law of the explorer Amerigo Vespucci, who gave America its name. She was considered the most beautiful woman in Florence, and the whole city mourned her when she died at only twenty-three years old.

Ghirlandaio
1448-1494

Domenico Ghirlandaio was about the same age as Botticelli, and they worked side-by-side in Florence and elsewhere. He is particularly known for his colorful wall paintings in several of Florence's churches.

It's Christmas night, and Ghirlandaio has painted the stable with Mary, Joseph, and the newborn child. Here is a manger, an ox, and a donkey, as well as shepherds and sheep. It is typical of the nativity scenes we see around Christmastime.

But if we look more closely, not everything is what we think it to be. First of all, this is not a stable but rather a Roman ruin with classical columns and a triumphal arch in the background. Ghirlandaio, like most artists in Florence at that time, studied ancient Rome, and he set the Christmas story in a Roman ruin. Perhaps that setting is a symbol in the painting? That the child is born into our broken world? What do we glimpse in the distance? Florence, the beautiful city—the new, reborn Rome.

The shepherds are no longer the stylized figures from the Middle Ages, who were often lined up, looking solemn, staff in hand. Now, they have become *real* shepherds. They are shabby and dirty (and probably smell bad and are full of lice). They were far down the social ladder, but they were the ones who got to see the child first.

By the way, have you noticed that one of the shepherds points to the child while gesturing towards himself with the other hand? This is Ghirlandaio himself. He has painted himself into the picture as a signature. A self-portrait, or, in more modern words, a "selfie."

The child is not in his mother's arms but lies on the ground, as if to symbolize that he does not belong to her, but to the whole earth. Joseph keeps watching as his hand rests on the empty manger. But wait a minute! Look one more time. It's not a manger at all, but a Roman *sarcophagus*, a coffin. It symbolizes what is to come, namely the child's death. But it also symbolizes the resurrection because the coffin is open and empty. We have Christmas and Easter in the same painting.

Domenico Ghirlandaio: *Adoration of the Shepherds*, 1483–1485. Church of Santa Trínita, Florence

Leonardo da Vinci
1452–1519

Leonardo arrived in Florence when he was about fifteen years old, beginning his apprenticeship in the workshop of a painter and sculptor named Verrocchio. Already as a young boy, Leonardo impressed everyone with his skills. It was not long before he surpassed his teacher and started receiving commissions on his own. He did not have much schooling but was eager to learn, curious, and always looking for new knowledge and new skills.

He was what we call a true *Renaissance man*, someone who masters many arts. He was a painter, sculptor, engineer, and inventor. If there was something he didn't know, he would find someone who could explain it to him, and he didn't move on until he understood.

Anatomy, physics, mathematics, biology, and chemistry. To him, everything was interesting. He was full of creative playfulness, but he also mastered analytical

Leonardo da Vinci: *Annunciation*, c. 1472–1476. Uffizi Gallery

thinking. He was an artist, but he also wanted to investigate and understand why things were the way they were—not just accept something as truth until he had examined it and seen that it was true.

Leonardo did not finish many paintings, but the few we know are truly great pieces of art.

One thing that especially sets Leonardo apart from other Renaissance artists is that he faithfully kept a journal. In his notebooks, we find everything from to-do lists to his thoughts about nature and society. He would also draw in these notebooks. He made sketches for future paintings or inventions. Over 7500 of his notebook pages have been preserved until this day!

He designed bicycles, airplanes, and helicopters hundreds of years before anyone even considered building them. We can safely say that he was ahead of his time.

The Annunciation is another common theme in art history. It focuses on the angel Gabriel appearing before Mary,

telling her that she will conceive and give birth to the son of God.

Leonardo da Vinci was only about twenty years old when he painted this picture, but we see what a master he already was.

Typically, artists would paint this theme with Mary humbly bowing her head, but in Leonardo's painting, she seems surprised (logically!) by the angel's visit, and probably not least by his words. It is as if she really wants to understand what is happening to her.

In this picture, Leonardo has followed the trend of painting the holy scene in a familiar setting because Mary is sitting outside a mansion that looks like those people would see in Tuscany. Viewers could recognize not only how the house was built but also the trees and flowers native to their region.

More Symbols

While talking of Fra Filippo Lippi, we learned about the symbolism of Mary's red dress and blue cloak, but if we still are

in doubt about who this girl is, Leonardo has thrown in several more hints to help us: *The blooming garden* is an ancient symbol of Mary. Do you see the flowers that Gabriel offers Mary? The *white lilies* symbolize her virginity. This is why bridal bouquets in many countries traditionally have consisted of white lilies.

In many Annunciation paintings, we see Mary holding a book in her hands or as here, seated at a reading desk. It is highly unlikely that a young woman in Nazareth knew how to read, but Leonardo, like so many other artists, often paints her reading, probably to show us that she was a thinking person and not just a "birthing machine." I like that idea. I want to go over to her and ask what she's reading or what she thinks about what that angel just told her.

Notice the background. Leonardo always took his time to paint this, that was often seen as less important, and he was very good at painting both landscape and details. On the horizon, we glimpse a port and a ship, and that could direct our

---

Some Math: The Golden Ratio

The golden ratio is also called *the mathematical formula for beauty*, and it became popular during the Renaissance. It's about dividing a line in two so that the ratio between the entire line and the longest part is the same as the ratio between the shortest part and the longest.

The golden ratio has, since antiquity, been used as a basis for the composition of images and architecture, and it has been perceived as a beautiful and harmonious way of dividing up an image surface.

The ratio also applies to rectangles and even spirals. We find the golden ratio in nature, in everything from pinecones, snail shells, and sunflowers to the human body and galaxies in space.

The golden ratio is often symbolized by the Greek letter ϕ (phi) and is an irrational number with a value of approximately 1.6.

$$a \qquad b$$

$$\frac{a+b}{a} = \frac{a}{b} = 1.61803 \ldots \qquad a+b$$

Leonardo da Vinci: *The Virgin and Child with Saint Anne*,
1501-1519. Louvre, Paris.

thoughts toward someone who is going on a journey, but then, of course, it depicts the contrary—someone is going to arrive.

Remember me saying that the Madonna and Child is the most used subject in all Western art history? Here is another version, painted by Leonardo da Vinci. We recognize Mary, with her red dress and the blue cloak, which slips off her shoulders, as she reaches out to pick up her toddler Jesus. But also, we see a third person in the painting. Mary sits on the lap of her mother, Anne.

Little Jesus holds a lamb, yet another symbol: In the times of the Old Testament, young lambs were sacrificed to God, but Jesus became the new sacrificial lamb through his suffering and death. He became the "Lamb of God."

Leonardo painted this picture towards the end of his life, but he did not quite finish it. The background remains at the sketch stage, but the picture is still considered one of the most beautiful examples of Renaissance art, full of harmony. You can rest your eyes on a picture like this for a long time without

getting tired, and one of the reasons is that Leonardo used the golden ratio. (See "The Golden Ratio" on p.44.) Mary's face is approximately in the golden ratio of the image, and this means that no matter where we try to fix our gaze, sooner or later we will be drawn back to her eyes.

This painting doesn't hang in the Uffizi Gallery but in the Louvre. You might ask why, and the answer is simple: Towards the end of his life, the French King, Francis I, invited Leonardo to be his court painter. Leonardo accepted and ended up living the rest of his life in France. He left behind several paintings, both finished and unfinished, and this is why several of his works of art are now in the Louvre in Paris. The Louvre was the king's palace then and did not become an art gallery until several hundred years later.

In the Louvre, as mentioned, we can also enjoy the world-famous *La Gioconda*, or *Mona Lisa,* as she is known in most of the world. This portrait of a young woman from Florence, famous for the woman's mysterious smile, has taken on a life of its own.

Leonardo Da Vinci: *Mona Lisa*, 1503-06. Louvre, Paris

Michelangelo
1475–1562

Michelangelo Buonarroti grew up in Florence, where he also lived for a large part of his life. He was a generation younger than Leonardo, and in contrast to the older artist, who was popular and outgoing, Michelangelo is often described as withdrawn and aloof, and he was seen as both a bit odd and difficult. As a child, he experienced tremendous loss and grief, which probably scarred him for life.

Michelangelo was, like Leonardo, a true Renaissance man. He was an engineer, architect, painter, and poet. But what was closest to his heart was carving sculptures in stone, and despite having little education in that area, he quickly became a master at this art.

Michelangelo worked in a way that basically no one else has ever done. Where other sculptors first form their sculptures in something soft, like clay or plaster, then use this as a template when carving in stone, Michelangelo simply set to work with a hammer and chisel, directly on the marble, without a template or any other kind of help.

"The sculpture is already there inside the rock," he said. "All I have to do is remove what shouldn't be there." He described the process as a person rising from the water, appearing little by little.

Michelangelo's most famous work in Florence is the colossal sculpture depicting David from the Old Testament. This theme is also common in art history: the story about the shepherd boy David, who joined the war and defeated the giant Goliath with the help of a slingshot and a stone.

The authorities in Florence wanted this David statue as a symbol of their small city, which always seemed to stand up to the big cities surrounding it. For several hundred years, the statue of David stood in the Signoria, outside Florence's old town hall, but in the nineteenth century, the statue was moved into the gallery of the Art Academy of Florence, where a separate room was built for it. The statue itself measures thirteen feet, but if we include the base on which David stands, the work of art rises over sixteen feet!

It is hard to grasp that this sculpture is carved from a single piece of marble. Notice the muscles, the blood vessels on the back of his hand, and the fingernails. And see how Michelangelo has depicted emotions. If we study David's face, we see fear and uncertainty, but also courage and willpower.

David defeating Goliath is a well-known theme in art history. Most artists would show David as a teenager, either shy, with a lowered gaze, or boisterous and self-confident. And it was customary to show him after he had killed Goliath, with the giant's head on the ground.

Michelangelo, on the contrary, has chosen to give us David *before* he slays the giant while he still has the stone in one hand. And instead of a teenager, he is a fully grown man, looking like a Greek god. After all, Michelangelo was a true Renaissance man, greatly inspired by the sculptures of antiquity, and his sculptural art was to become the norm for hundreds of years onward.

Michelangelo: *David*, 1501–1504.
Galleria dell'Accademia, Florence

St. Peter's Basilica. Rome

Michelangelo lived a large part of his adult life in Rome, where he carried out large works commissioned by the Pope. Among other things, he constructed the dome of St. Peter's Basilica, and he painted the ceiling of the Sistine Chapel. For four years, Michelangelo lay on his back on a scaffold under the ceiling, where he painted biblical scenes, prophets, and ornaments. During these years, he wrote letters, complaining about how exhausted he was and how boring he found this work.

The Creation of Adam is clearly the most famous detail from this ceiling. Later, Michaelangelo was commissioned to also paint one of the end walls of the chapel. There, the theme would be Judgment Day.

But despite Michelangelo's skill as a painter and architect, it was, as mentioned, the art of sculpture that was closest to his heart. Now let's view what is considered the world's most beautiful marble statue.

If you enter the main entrance of St. Peter's Basilica and turn right, you will see it. *The Pietà* (Latin for *mourning* or *lamentation*) is another common theme in Western art history. In the sculpture, Mary no longer holds her little child in her arms, but rather her grown, lifeless son right after he was taken down from the cross.

Michelangelo's *Pietà* is human-sized, and as in the David sculpture, the realism is striking. Admire the draping robes, the perfect anatomy. It is almost difficult to believe that this is hard marble. The

Sistine Chapel, Vatican

Michelangelo: *The Creation of Adam*. The ceiling of the Sistine Chapel, Vatican

Michelangelo: *The Pietà*, 1498–1499. St. Peter's Basilica, Rome

detailed sculpting makes you want to touch Mary's cloak because you cannot accept that this is not soft fabric.

But more than anything else, it is amazing how Michelangelo, a young man at 22, could set grief in stone. Look at Mary's posture and facial expression, which tell us that she is destroyed by grief. "How on earth will I be able to go on living now?" she must be thinking.

Grief is part of human life. It's something we all will experience sooner or later. That a young man, over five hundred years ago, knew these feelings and had the ability to show them—in hard rock—can help us. We are reminded that we are not alone and that what we feel is not unique. Other people experience something similar. Our grief may not be the same as Mary's, but still, our feelings can be similar, and this sculpture can bring relief and comfort, whether we see it in real life or depicted in a book, as you are doing right now.

Raphael
1483-1520

Raffaello Sanzio was his name, that young man from Urbino who became famous while working in Rome at the beginning of the sixteenth century. He was eight years younger than Michelangelo, and over thirty years younger than Leonardo da Vinci. He is often called the "Madonna painter," because he is particularly known for his beautiful paintings of the Virgin Mary with baby Jesus.

Raphael died at age thirty-seven, and all of Rome mourned the loss of the talented artist, who was also known as a pleasant young man and a good person. On his tomb (in the Pantheon of Rome), you can read this sentence: "Here lies Raphael, by whom nature herself feared to be outdone while he lived, and when he died, feared that she herself would die."

In the *Madonna del Granduca*, Raphael has removed all the background, so only the central theme remains, Mary with little Jesus. Red dress and blue cape, naked baby—everything is simple but also perfect. No more is needed when Raphael holds the paintbrush.

But he also painted other versions of Mary and the Child, such as *Madonna in the Chair*. In this painting, Mary is dressed in contemporary fashion from Rome, and she sits in a chair with the baby in her arms. Here Jesus looks like a chubby one-year-old.

The picture is a *tondo*, meant to hang over a doorway, and the way the picture is painted reinforces this perspective. We already have the feeling of being underneath the picture, looking up at it.

Raphael: *Madonna del Granduca*. 1505. Galleria Palatina, Florence

Raphael: *Madonna della Seggiola (Madonna in the Chair)*. 1513-14. Galleria Palatina, Florence

Next to Mary and the child, we can see little John the Baptist. He was Jesus's cousin, and he is also considered a forerunner to him, preaching to people and asking them to repent from their sinful ways. John pointed to Jesus and called him the "Lamb of God." In the Bible, we can read about John retreating into the wilderness, dressed only in a cloak made of camel's hair, eating nothing but wild honey and grasshoppers. This is why, although, in this picture, he is a small

Raphael: *The Deposition*. 1507. Galleria Borghese, Rome

child, he is depicted wearing a camel's hair cloak and holding a walking stick shaped like a cross. The little child already worships Jesus with folded hands.

If you were to travel to Rome one day, you could enter the beautiful park of Villa Borghese, north of the city center, where you will find the Borghese Gallery, a real gem of a museum. Not too big, but with many wonderful things to see! The building itself is a beautiful palace decorated in the Baroque style. (Read about the Baroque period in Chapter 5.)

On the second floor, we can admire Raphael's painting, where the dead Christ is taken down from the cross. The three empty crosses can be seen in the background. Many people are present at the scene, but the painting is still not crowded. Raphael knows perfectly well what he is doing. Each individual is placed exactly where he or she should be. The picture has balance, and it has harmony, despite the fact that the scene is heartbreakingly sad.

Mary, the mother of Jesus, is to the right. She has fainted and is now being helped by three women. At the top left, we see the young disciple John, the one whom Jesus asked to care for Mary, to consider as his own mother. John is grieving, but the person who, more than any other, shows her pain and grief is Mary Magdalene. She, who probably was one of Jesus's closest friends, is completely dissolved in grief. She holds his hand, and it looks as if she refuses to accept the fact that her friend is dead and is begging him to wake up. If we look closely, we can even spot a teardrop on her cheek. The artist has worked according to the golden ratio (see p. 44), and no matter where we fix our gaze, our eyes will end up on her, the grieving Mary Magdalene.

Titian
1488/90–1576

Tiziano Vecellio (Titian in English) is considered the most important representative of the Renaissance in Venice. He was born in Pieve di Cadore but came to Venice as a young boy, and this city became his home for most of his life.

He is the leader of what we call the Venetian school. When we use the word *school* in art history, we do not mean a school in the physical sense but a method, a way of painting. And Titian's school, or method, is about color. For him, color was more important than the drawing. He is regarded as the first modern painter, though he lived several hundred years before we begin to call painting *modern*.

The beautiful painting "Venus of Urbino" is located in the Uffizi Gallery, and once again, we meet the goddess of love, Venus. No naked woman lies here, but rather Love itself in human form, just like Botticelli's image of the birth of Venus on p. 61.

Titian portrays Venus as a noble young woman resting on a bed or sofa, waiting for her chambermaids to dress her. The sheet has been pulled aside so that we see the red color of the mattress underneath. Red symbolizes, among other things, love and passion. This color can be found in many of Titian's pictures.

Do you see the sleeping dog at her feet? Just as in van Eyck's engagement picture, the dog symbolizes loyalty and devotion, qualities of true love. Titian was an artist who became a great inspiration for painters who came after him, and over three hundred years later, Manet, in France, would paint a version of this picture that was not well received. People found it inappropriate and unpleasant to view. More on that later.

Titian: *Venus of Urbino*, 1532–1534. Uffizi Gallery, Florence

Bronzino
1503-1572

Agnolo Bronzino is primarily known as a portrait painter in the sixteenth century. In his portraits, typically, nothing appears in the background. Behind the person is a monochrome surface, with a light aimed at the models he paints. Perhaps Bronzino's pictures inspired the traditional backdrops of modern-day portrait photographers. In any case, he was ahead of his time, as plain backgrounds only became popular in the Baroque period, which we will examine in the next chapter.

Bronzino received many commissions from the Grand Duke of Tuscany, Cosimo I de' Medici. He painted the Grand Duke himself, his wife Eleonora, and all their children. Many of these portraits may be seen today in the Uffizi Gallery.

Notice this little girl. Her name was Bia de' Medici, and she was the daughter of the Grand Duke of Tuscany. She was an illegitimate child (a terrible word, by the way), born before the Grand Duke married. We don't know who her mother was, but she was probably a village girl at one of the family's many villas in the countryside.

Bia was taken from her mother immediately after birth because despite being born out of wedlock, she was nevertheless a Medici, and the family took the infant with them to Florence. She was then placed with her paternal grandmother. The little girl fell ill and died at only five years old, and it was reported that the Grand Duke deeply mourned the loss of his first child. The portrait of Bia hangs side by side with his other children in the Uffizi Gallery.

Bronzino: *Bia de' Medici*, c. 1542.
Uffizi Gallery, Florence

Parmigianino
1503–1540

Formally named Girolamo Francesco Maria Mazzola, this Renaissance painter was called Parmigianino because he came from the city of Parma. I guess we could call him Mr. Parmesan, which makes me smile.

This picture was painted during the mid-sixteenth century, and it belongs to the style we call *mannerism*. It's still Renaissance, but this style is different from the Renaissance we have seen so far. The composition is somehow off balance, with empty space to the right and a cluster of figures to the left. Furthermore, the painting is not realistic, with Mary's excessively long neck and the child's body being unnaturally long.

Many art historians don't like this style. It has been considered artificial, made up, stylized, and removed from reality, but if you give this painting a chance, you will see a lot unfolding before your eyes. Some of the figures look like eager, impatient children. On the empty side of the painting, there is only one single figure: a motionless man in the background, holding up a scroll. Maybe a prophet? What we first see on the right, a lonely column, is actually a colonnade, a whole row of columns rising towards the sky, where dark clouds gather, perhaps foreshadowing the storm that will come in this child's life.

Notice also how Mary is sitting and how the child is stretched out across her lap, pale and lifeless. This portrayal makes me think of a *Pietà*, that is, Mary with the dead Christ on her lap (see page 54).

I think Parmigianino did this on purpose. By letting the child remind us of the dead Christ, he triggers emotions in us.

Emotion is one of the characteristics of the next era we'll head into, the Baroque.

Parmigianino: *Madonna with the Long Neck,*
1535-1540. Uffizi Gallery, Florence

CHAPTER 5

Baroque

The Art during the Baroque period changed from the Renaissance in several ways. Typical elements of this art are storytelling, drama, and movement.

When we talk about the Baroque, we usually mean the seventeenth century and the first half of the eighteenth century. *Baroque* means *irregular pearl*, and it was originally used as an insult, a synonym for *ugly* or even *grotesque*.

And for a long time, art historians agreed that art from this period was ugly, that the Baroque period was a mistake, and that the break with the harmony of the Renaissance was a disaster. But little by little, opinions changed, and art historians started viewing the Baroque as an era with its own beauty while still carrying on the best of the Renaissance.

But it's true that baroque art changed Europe. Just look at architecture from this period. While Renaissance buildings were characterized by clean lines, an understated harmony, and balance, baroque came with opulence. Churches and palaces were now heavily decorated, embellishments completely covering walls and ceilings, and large quantities of marble and gold were used. It's almost as if baroque buildings are calling out at us: "Look at me!"

The Counter-Reformation

The opulence of baroque art can be largely explained as a reaction to the Reformation, that is, when the Christian church was split. The Reformation was a major crisis in the history of art. The reformed churches did not want art at all, or at least very little, and the number of artist commissions dropped. A few artists could make a living by painting portraits for the upper class as well as the occasional altarpiece, but most painters and sculptors had to find another profession.

In Italy and the rest of Catholic Europe, the opposite happened. There, the *Counter-Reformation* began, and art flourished more than ever! One can almost imagine the Catholics saying: "If you guys don't want art, we're going to have even

Piazza Navona in Rome is typical of Baroque architecture

more than before." Counter-Reformation and Baroque thus go together. The churches become full, even overflowing with works of art, and this also goes for private and public palaces, squares, fountains, and parks. It's lavish and over-the-top but beautifully splendid.

Bernini
1598-1680

When it comes to Renaissance sculpture, Michelangelo is considered the greatest of that era, and if we are to mention only one sculptor from the Baroque period, it has to be Giovanni Lorenzo Bernini. He was the leading sculptor and architect in Rome during the seventeenth century, and he definitely put his mark on the city through buildings, decorations, and free-standing artworks.

In the Borghese Gallery, a wonderful art gallery in the Borghese Park, we find Bernini's *David*. And yes, it's the same David featured in Michelangelo's sculpture (see p. 49), but Bernini has chosen to depict him differently.

David looks younger here, and he is determined and full of youthful resolve. He is gritting his teeth as he charges with his slingshot. While the Renaissance emphasized beauty, calm, and harmony, the Baroque period is characterized by movement and drama. To put it simply: Michelangelo's David stands still, but this one certainly does not. He is poised to throw that rock. Bernini has captured the movement as if a film has been paused, and if you find yourself in front of this sculpture, you'll want to take a step to the side for fear of that rock hitting you in the middle of your face.

The sculpture you see below and on the previous pages 70 and 71 is also in the Borghese Gallery of Rome, and like the *David* statue, this one is full of movement and drama. It describes a story from Greek mythology: Proserpina, goddess of spring, was picking flowers in a field when Hades, lord of the underworld, caught sight of her. He wanted her, and he didn't listen to her saying no, instead he dragged her down into his kingdom. All the flowers of the earth withered. Her mother, Demeter, mourned and searched for her. At last, she found her daughter in the underworld, and full of joy, she brought her home. The flowers grew again on Earth. But Persephone had accepted and eaten six pomegranate seeds, and because of that act, she was forever condemned to spend six months of the year with Hades in the underworld. The myth thus explains the change of seasons.

Gian Lorenzo Bernini: *David*, 1623-1624. Galleria Borghese, Rome

Gian Lorenzo Bernini: *The Rape of Proserpina*,
1621-1622. Galleria Borghese, Rome

Bernini's sculpture is certainly dramatic. We see Hades as he grabs Persephone, and we have to remind ourselves that this is marble, not human bodies. We can see Hades's strong muscles, how his whole body tightens, his fingers squeezing into Persephone's thighs. She tries in vain to free herself, and in her face, we see wild anxiety—and two marble tears.

Gian Lorenzo Bernini: *The Rape of Proserpina*, 1621-1622.
Galleria Borghese, Rome

Guido Reni
1575–1642

Reni was from Bologna, but he moved to Rome around the year 1600. He is especially known for his beautiful portraits, biblical characters, and mythological motifs.

Scholars now dispute whether it is Reni who painted this picture, or whether it was one of these two: *Elisabetta Sirani*, who was the daughter of one of his apprentices, or *Ginevra Cantofoli*, a contemporary artist in Bologna. Women in art history have often been overlooked, hidden in the dark, and forgotten, and sometimes men have been given credit for their artwork. Guido Reni has, until recently, been considered the artist behind this portrait, but I choose to give one of the women the benefit of the doubt. Personally, I think it is the more unknown Ginevra.

If you get to see this small painting in Rome's Palazzo Barberini, you'll experience something strange. It is impossible to walk by without stopping. It's as if her gaze begs you to come over to her, to listen to her story.

The portrait is typical of the Baroque period, as there is no background. During the Renaissance, the background was important, but here we see only a diffused darkness behind the beautiful portrait. Something else typical of baroque art is that there is a story. Something is happening, despite Beatrice's apparent calmness.

Her story is horrific. Beatrice was a young Roman girl who was abused by her father for years. At one point, she was locked up in a room, completely at the mercy of the man. Finally, she couldn't take it anymore, and with the help of one of her brothers and a servant, she had her father killed. But the evidence pointed towards Beatrice, and she was arrested and sentenced to death.

The people of Rome were in an uproar. Everyone knew what had been going on, but her father was powerful, and nobody knew how to help her. Although they agreed that she should be pardoned, they could do nothing about it. She was beheaded on September 11, 1599, by the Castel Sant' Angelo, where the bridge Ponte Sant' Angelo begins.

Until recently, it was thought that the picture was painted in the hope of changing her sentence, but perhaps it was painted decades later, as a tribute to Beatrice. We don't have the answer, but we do have the beautiful painting.

Do you remember the quote from Chekhov, that the role of the artist is to ask questions? (Page 15) What the painter gives us here is beauty, tragedy, and many, many questions.

Beatrice Cenci, painted c. 1600 - perhaps by Guido Reni?

Caravaggio
1571–1610

The name of this artist was actually Michelangelo di Merisi (yes, the same first name as the one we already talked about), but he was nicknamed Caravaggio because he came from the village of Caravaggio, not far from Milan. He moved to Rome towards the end of the sixteenth century. After initially working for others, painting fruit platters, flowers, in short, everything that was considered less important, his talent was eventually discovered, and he started to get his own commissions. He quickly became both in demand and debated because, despite being an outstanding painter, his style was too different from what people were used to seeing. That art should be realistic had been important since the Renaissance, but the general view was that Caravaggio's realism went too far. Sometimes his patrons refused the paintings, and he had to start over again, which made him furious! He was, however, relentless in staying close to reality, both in the beautiful and the ugly, and today we typically use words like "photographically correct" when we talk about Caravaggio's paintings.

He lived a dramatic life. As a child, he survived a plague epidemic, and he witnessed much misery and death. As an adult, he was often involved in trouble, in and out of jail, and even accused of murder. He died of illness at age thirty-nine. But despite the fact that his career lasted only about a decade, he managed to change the art of painting. He is the first one to employ what we call *chiaroscuro*, an Italian expression meaning light-dark. His pictures are often marked by darkness, but there is always a bright light showing us what is important and what to focus on. His paintings may have us think of a darkened theater stage, where a spotlight is aimed at the actors.

In Caravaggio's altarpiece, *Madonna di Loreto,* we once again see the Virgin Mary with Jesus, here being a child of 2–3 years. The painting caused a stir because Caravaggio chose to place Mary in the doorway of what looked like an apartment building in Rome at the time. In a painting like this, Mary becomes one of us, as if she were the woman next door, maybe getting her son ready for bed, when there was a knock on the door, and she had to go out with the naked child in her arms. Here she is, astonished to see the pilgrims who have come to worship her offspring.

That Caravaggio was a great painter was certain, but there was disagreement about whether such a picture was suitable in a church. Many thought that realism had gone way too far. The plaster is peeling off the wall, and Mary stands barefoot in the doorway. This was no way to portray the Virgin Mary—it wasn't respectful, not holy enough. Not to mention the pilgrims' dirty feet, which are at the very front of the picture. Dirty feet—in a church?

Today, we can appreciate his relentless realism. The house is not perfect; the pilgrims are poor and dirty. Mary is barefoot, she is a tired young mother, and because of this, we can relate to her. She has been taken down from the pedestal and has become one of us.

Examine the artist's use of light and shadow. The picture is very dark, yet a spotlight shines on Mary and the child. Notice then that the child himself has become a source of light because the light also shines from him onto the pilgrims.

Caravaggio: *Madonna di Loreto*, 1604.
Church of San Agostino, Rome

Let's keep walking a little further north, to Piazza del Popolo. Just below the Pincio hill, we find the Basilica of Santa Maria del Popolo, and inside, in a small chapel, you will see this painting by Caravaggio, which is about St. Paul's conversion.

You can read about this story in the Bible, in the New Testament. Paul (known as Saul at this time) was a zealous official, agreeing with the authorities that the Christians were causing unnecessary turmoil and confusion. These weirdos claimed that Jesus of Nazareth had risen from the dead. He agreed that it was best to stop them and restore peace and order. Paul was probably convinced he was doing the right thing as he headed to Damascus to arrest some Christians there. Suddenly, a bright light came out of the sky and blinded him. He heard a voice saying, "Why are you persecuting me?" (Acts 9:4, ESV)

Incidentally, shortly after this event, we hear no more about Paul, not until around two years later, when he reappears, transformed into an ardent advocate for Christianity. Today, we consider him the first Christian missionary, as he traveled around the world, founding churches.

Caravaggio was commissioned to paint this scene, and he imagined St. Paul falling from his horse. Perhaps the horse became frightened and bolted? In any case, the picture is very unusual. Paul is lying on the ground, and the point of view in the picture is such that we could be Paul looking up at the confused horse. Also, notice how Caravaggio uses the light. We can't see the light source itself, but we see that it comes from above and that it illuminates Paul's face.

How shocked the churchgoers must have been when they saw this picture for the first time, where the rear end of a horse covers a large part of the painting!

Once again, I must say that today we probably understand Caravaggio much better than people did in the seventeenth century. He makes this Bible story understandable! Instead of painting an angel or the face of God in the sky, he paints a young man who has fallen from his horse and is lying on the ground. It's down to earth, literally. The sacred becomes tangible.

Caravaggio is a good example of how the best artists are often ahead of their time; they are not appreciated until long after their death. Only in the twentieth century was Caravaggio recognized among art historians and the general public.

Caravaggio: *Conversion of St. Paul*, 1600.
Santa Maria del Popolo, Rome

Vermeer
1632-1675

Let's go to the Netherlands. What was going on there during this time?

We talked about how the Reformation became a crisis for many artists. The church had been the most important employer of the artists, and because the newly founded Protestant church did not want art, many painters and sculptors had to find a new profession. An exception to this was the Protestant areas of the Netherlands, where art flourished in the seventeenth century. We even call it the Dutch Golden Age.

The Netherlands had become an independent nation, free from the Spanish king, and fierce optimism spread throughout the country. In a few decades, Amsterdam multiplied in size, and Dutch cities were the center of world trade. Out of this trade emerged a new group of individuals: rich merchants. These people wanted to buy art, and they weren't necessarily interested in Bible stories or pictures of saints. They often wanted paintings that showed ordinary people doing ordinary things, like writing letters, playing musical instruments, talking, or cooking. This type of art, which today we call *genre painting*, would often contain an element of humor, and there was often a message or a moral embedded in it.

The painter Johannes Vermeer came from the city of Delft, where he lived all his life. He is one of the most known representatives of Dutch baroque art.

In the picture that we call *The Glass of Wine*, we enter a Dutch home in the seventeenth century. Vermeer was a master when it came to painting beautiful interiors. Notice the leaded glass window, the tiled floor, the beautifully carved chair,

Johannes Vermeer: *The Glass of Wine*, 1660. Gemäldegalerie, Berlin

and the Persian rug that doubles as a tablecloth. This is a snapshot of a typical Dutch home at the time. Also, notice his excellent use of light. Vermeer was very much a master of light, although he uses it in a softer way than Caravaggio. See how the light comes from the window, illuminating the young woman and sparkling in the glass.

But keep in mind; this is not just a lovely interior with a woman drinking wine. The man is serving the wine, but he has neither taken off his hat nor his cloak, and he has not sat down. There is something unsettling about him. As if he is in a hurry? And while the young woman's face is illuminated, the man's face is in shadow from the broad hat brim. Does he have something to hide? He stares at the young woman as she drinks, and he has a good grip on that wine jug. He must be waiting for her to finish her glass, and then he will immediately pour another one. Have you noticed the string instrument on the chair and the sheet music on the table? He clearly intends to play for her when she has finished the wine. He has an agenda. And here is a subtle message to us viewers: young women should beware of men who serve them wine. Especially when the man doesn't bother to take off his hat.

The portrait, now known as *Girl with a Pearl Earring*, and which was previously called *Girl with a Turban*, is located in the Mauritshuis, a wonderful museum in the beautiful city of The Hague, Netherlands.

The picture clearly differs from Vermeer's other works, which are mostly interiors with people being busy with some kind of task. In this painting, however, we only have the portrait of a girl with a dark background. She is dressed in a strange way, very different from Dutch women in the 1600s.

I have a theory about how this picture came to be: A merchant from the Netherlands came to Rome and saw the portrait of Beatrice Cenci (see p. 73), which had been painted a few decades earlier. He was thrilled, and when he returned to the Netherlands, he sought out Vermeer and asked him to reproduce the painting: A young woman with a turban on her head, looking over her shoulder. Dark background. Vermeer painted two different versions of the picture with two different models. This has clearly become the most famous of Vermeer's pictures, and it has largely taken on a life of its own.

The painting became particularly famous when Tracy Chevalier wrote her novel *Girl with a Pearl Earring*, in which she composed a story about how the painting came to be. The book is delightful, and a beautiful, toned-down movie of the same name was made afterward, but keep in mind that this is fiction. We know very little about Vermeer's life and have no idea who this woman is. And maybe this is exactly what has made the picture so famous. Is that a smile we see, or is she distressed? Afraid maybe? She is mysterious, and we can try to understand her, but we will never know for sure.

Perhaps we can find answers in ourselves while we look at her. While we admire the beautiful colors. The textures. The light. Or perhaps we should allow ourselves to enjoy the painting without needing to understand. We can let the mystery be just that, make room for wonder!

Johannes Vermeer: *Girl with a Pearl Earring*, 1665.
Mauritshuis, The Hague

Rembrandt
1606-1669

Rembrandt van Rijn came from the city of Leiden, Netherlands, and he became a painter, despite his father's preference for him to choose another profession. At age 13, he left school and began an apprenticeship with an artist in his hometown. Later he moved to Amsterdam, where he did very well, was commissioned by the city's authorities, and for years he made a good living from his art.

The huge painting (nearly 16.5 feet wide) depicting a company of Amsterdam's city guard getting ready for duty is called *The Night Watch*, simply because it has darkened over the years. Getting such an official commission was important socially but no less profitable for Rembrandt. And he went about this task in his own way. Normally, when setting up such a group picture, one would line up the men in rows (like a class picture), but Rembrandt has painted them as they are getting ready to march out, and it is as if they don't even know they are being painted. It's all slightly chaotic and rich in detail. If you take some time, you will keep discovering things in this painting.

Rembrandt married Saskia, the love of his life, and they had four children. For a while, he was happy, but then fate was cruel to him. Three out of four children died in infancy, and Titus, the only one who grew up, died at age twenty-six. And by then, Saskia had already passed away.

Rembrandt van Rijn: *The Night Watch*, 1642.
Rijksmuseum, Amsterdam

This picture was painted towards the end of Rembrandt's life and shows how much his style changed. The paintings became more "woolly," like a precursor of impressionism, which would come two hundred years later.

The story of *The Return of the Prodigal Son* is taken from the Bible: A father had two sons. The youngest requested his share of the inheritance, and then he went off and spent it all on, let's say, bad choices. When the money was gone, he became a beggar to survive, and in the end, he chose to return home, broke, miserable, diseased, and probably full of lice. He asked his father to be a servant in his house, as he believed that he no longer deserved to be a son. But the father was overjoyed to have his child back, and he embraced him and showered him with love. Not one word of criticism (Luke 15:11-32, ESV).

Now, notice the man on the right side of the picture. That's the older brother. He looks angry. He had done everything right. He stayed with his father, helping him and doing as he was told. And now, his father is making all this fuss because of that rascal of a little brother.

I think we can relate to the elder brother's feelings. The feeling of injustice.

The father's unconditional love, on the other hand, is more than we can relate to if we are honest. It's too good to be true. After all, that boy had behaved very badly!

But now I want you to look at the father's hands. Do you see that Rembrandt painted them differently? There is a man's hand and a woman's hand. Through this not-so-subtle hint, the artist reminds us that the story is not really about a man but about God, who loves his children unconditionally, no matter how they behave. And, to insinuate that God just as well could be a mother was highly controversial.

After Rembrandt's art changed, he received fewer commissions. In the end, he was not only lonely and heartbroken but also impoverished and sick, and when he died at sixty-six years old, his death was hardly noticed.

Nevertheless, today Rembrandt is considered the greatest artist of the Netherlands. He was another artist ahead of his time, and maybe that's why it became so difficult for him. This repeats throughout the history of art. Many of the best were misunderstood by their contemporaries, and they only became known as great artists long after their death.

Rembrandt van Rijn: *The Return of the Prodigal Son*, 1668. The Hermitage, St. Petersburg

CHAPTER 6

Rococo

The Palace of Versailles

The year is 1750, and we are at the Palace of Versailles, southwest of Paris. King Louis XV is on the throne, and the palace is filled with men and women in white wigs, tights, and high heels.

What we call Rococo was the eighteenth-century style, characterized by intricate architecture and furniture design, decorations, glitter, and gold. We could say that the baroque stretched to the extreme. Opulence had no limits during those years, and that also applied to consumption—for those who could afford it. The upper class lived in their own padded world, filled with palaces, parties, beautiful clothes, and art, while they held on to romantic dreams of a simple life in the countryside. They wanted paintings that showed country folk, often shepherds and shepherdesses, enjoying outdoor life, dressed in beautiful clothes, and keeping bow-decorated sheep on a leash. There should usually be some flirting involved or at least hints of romance. The upper class nurtured this fantasy, completely ignoring that reality

François Boucher: *Les Charmes de la Vie Champetre*, 1750. Accorsi-Ometto Museum, Turin.

was very different for most people in the country, with poverty, hunger, and despair. That those real-life shepherds lived in misery was not something the art-buying public wanted to know.

Boucher
1703–1770

François Boucher is one of the most important painters of this time. He made decent living painting portraits for the nobles of France, and he painted countless of the *pastorals* we mentioned previously, that is, paintings where shepherd boys and girls are staged in nature.

He made this pastoral scene around 1750. The landscape is beautiful and lush, and the shepherd boy and girls are dressed as if they were aristocrats at the Palace of Versailles, with expensive leather shoes, large dresses, and elaborate hairstyles.

The shepherd boy is clearly interested in one of the girls, who raises a finger at him, perhaps not quite convincingly. The other girl is a chaperone. She looks after the sheep and wants to assure us that everything is going well. For the moment, at least. And, really, those sheep with collars and bows!

The fountain in the background was a popular detail that patrons requested in paintings. It represented a fountain of love and the fantasy that if the young people would drink from it, they would fall hopelessly in love, unable to resist each other.

The painting below, *The Odalisque*, needs no interpretation or explanation. Such pictures were also highly in demand among the rich, art-buying people in France at the time. If they had such a painting hanging in one of their living rooms, they could, if they wanted, draw a curtain in front of it so that only select guests could see it.

François Boucher: *The Odalisque*, 1745. Louvre, Paris

Fragonard
1732–1806

Jean-Honoré Fragonard is another painter representing the French Rococo period. As with Boucher, we find among his paintings many of the "flirty pictures," which were so popular among the upper class.

Take a look at *The Lock*. A man and a woman are in a bedroom. The man is in his underwear, and while having a firm grip around the woman with one hand, he extends the other hand to lock the door. She tries to stop him, but her resistance is not convincing. Then go ahead and notice the red draperies. The use of red as a symbol of love and passion is almost too much here.

The upper classes loved such paintings and thought they were entertaining. Today we may ask ourselves some questions about what *really* is happening in the picture. Is this a loving couple, or is this disturbing to view?

Jean-Honoré Fragonard: *The Lock*, 1777.
Louvre, Paris

CHAPTER 7

The Nineteenth Century in France and the Many New Faces of Art

As we continued into the nineteenth century, art changed once again. The Age of Enlightenment and the Industrial Revolution introduced new thoughts and ideas. Little by little, we moved into a completely new reality where several painting styles existed side-by-side. We will look at some of these styles, but it is important to note that, from now on, there is no longer only one dominant style. Art is now about to enter the *modern era*, where artists would, to a much greater extent, decide what they want to paint. And it also becomes increasingly difficult to label the artists because they tended to work within several different styles during their artistic careers. We will deal with Romanticism, Realism, and Impressionism, but first, we have to talk about the "correct" way to paint in the 1800s. This is the style preferred by the authorities and the official art world. We call it Neoclassicism.

Neoclassicism

In neoclassic art, it's as if the Renaissance never ended. The classic motifs and the standards that were set during the Renaissance have not been forgotten, even though the motifs have changed, and artistic expression has taken new directions.

Around 1800, there is a renewed interest in both classical motifs and the traditional way of painting pictures. The paintings are large and magnificent; the surfaces are smooth, with no visible brush strokes. The motifs are harmonious, beautiful, and realistic—just as we saw in Renaissance paintings.

David
1748–1825

Jacques-Louis David is one of the greatest representatives of Neoclassicism, the style that was to become dominant for many decades. Though art began to adopt several styles, the art-buying public still preferred this classical style.

David was, above all, Napoleon Bonaparte's portrait painter. He painted countless pictures of the emperor: in the office, in uniform, and on horseback on his way across the Alps.

This enormous canvas measures nearly thirty-three feet in length. The large format gives us a feeling of being present at the scene in the mighty Notre Dame Cathedral. We see Napoleon, who would not allow the pope to perform the symbolic act of coronation. Instead, he now grabs the crown himself and places it on his own head. He then crowns his wife Josephine as his empress. Napoleon wanted to be like the ancient Roman emperors, who were not only omnipotent but also considered gods. At the time of its creation, this picture was highly relevant, like a press photo. At the same time, it becomes classical, as Napoleon, through his actions and his view of himself, draws the lines back to classical antiquity. *The Coronation* set the standard for how painters would complete their works to be recognized in Paris in the nineteenth century.

Romanticism

Romanticism, as a period in art history, roughly corresponds to the years 1800–1850, and it is not about romantic love but rather about imagination and emotions given a greater placc in art. This applies to painting, literature, music, and philosophy.

The Salon

Since the end of the seventeenth century, an official, annual art exhibition had been held in Paris. The *Salon of Painting and Sculpture*, or simply *The Salon* (Le Salon in French), as it was called.

For the artists, it was ever important to have their work displayed at the salon. Being rejected was associated with shame, and the artists would receive few or no opportunities to be acknowledged and sell their art.

The Salon jury had a lot of power regarding what art was accepted and displayed. In the second half of the nineteenth century, artists resisted this power, and in 1880, the Salon was discontinued.

Art then art became free, for better and for worse. The artist was free to create what he or she wanted, but at the same time, it was difficult to make oneself visible, to become known.

The movement is considered a reaction to the heavy industrialization of the world; people yearned for the past, for everything natural.

The artistic style of this period is diverse, and the Romantic aspect reflects those differences. For some artists, the focus is on the internal, that is, emotions and poetry; for others, the focus is external, and it's nature itself they depict. And keep in mind; this was something quite unusual. During the Renaissance, there were no landscape paintings. Nature was always in the background of something more important. Now, during the Romantic period, landscape painting became increasingly popular. Maybe it was all the technical innovations that made people seek nature, a need to see forests, mountains, and seas.

Jacques-Louis David: *Coronation of Napoleon at Notre-Dame,* 1807. Louvre, Paris

Turner
1775–1851

J. M. W. Turner was one of the most famous Romantic painters from England. His paintings caused a sensation in his time, as they often lacked the clarity one was used to seeing. He viewed nature and interpreted it in his own way. This is how he brought Leonardo da Vinci's words to life: "Painting is poetry that can be seen, not heard."

Turner's image of a boat in a blizzard must have shocked contemporary audiences, with its wild brushstrokes and crazy waves. The painting feels abstract until we take a closer look and realize what is happening: A boat is caught in the storm. We see the forces of nature at work, but at the same time, we can choose to see a painting of inner turmoil, a storm of emotions in the life of a person.

> *Painting is poetry that can be seen, not heard.*
>
> —Leonardo da Vinci

J. M. W. Turner: *Boat in a Blizzard*, 1842. Tate Britain, London

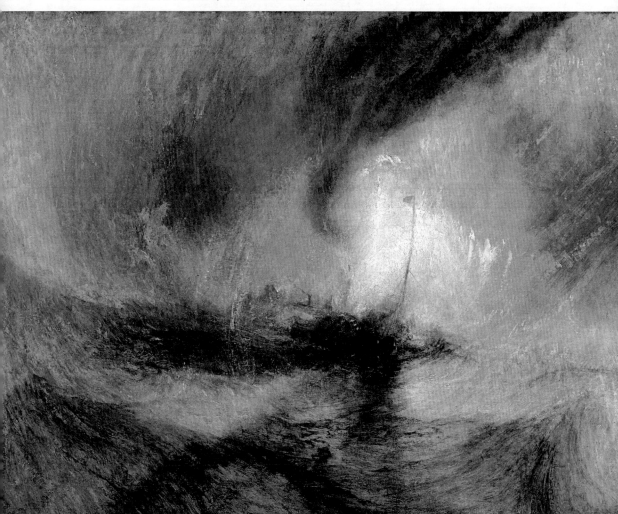

Eugène Delacroix: *Liberty Leading the People*, 1830. Louvre, Paris

Delacroix
1798–1863

Eugène Delacroix is one of the most important French Romantics. His approach to Romanticism was largely about country and people, politics, and society.

Even after the French Revolution in 1789, there were constant rebellions and revolutions in Paris. People still suffered injustice and misery, and they wanted what the French Revolution fought for: liberty, equality, and fraternity.

In this painting, we see an illustration of what is referred to as the July Revolution of 1830. We see corpses spread over a rough barricade, as well as people of different ages and classes with weapons in their hands, climbing, crawling, shouting, and fighting. The picture is an allegory, a picture describing an idea. There is no bare-breasted woman here—that lady is Liberty herself. Freedom in human shape dominates this painting. She lifts high *Le Tricolore*, the French national flag, and she wears the Phrygian cap, which during the French Revolution, became a symbol of freedom.

This painting has really lived a life of its own. From 1979 to 1997, it could be seen on the French one hundred-franc note, and it also inspired the stage design for the musical *Les Misérables*.

Both Turner and Delacroix dared to paint in a whole new way, where not all contours were sharp, where areas were left to the imagination. This would, to a great extent, inspire the impressionists only a few decades later.

Realism

As we move further into the nineteenth century, art changes once again. And now, as I mentioned earlier, it changes in several directions at once. While some artists still paint classical pictures, biblical scenes, and portraits, others have been inspired by the Romantic currents and paint nature or emotional pictures.

However, around 1850, Realism entered the art scene as a reaction to Romanticism. The term doesn't mean painting "photographically correct," but that the *motifs* should be realistic and showcase the real world. These artists wanted to paint reality as it was, preferably the dark sides of society, the social differences, and how poor people lived.

For painters to use their art as social criticism was new, and it was not always well received by those who had the money to buy art, namely the upper classes.

Millet
1814–1875

Jean-François Millet is one of the most famous Realists in France, although he can easily fit on other "shelves" as well. In the 1800s, remember, it is not as easy to say that a painter is only this or that. Several styles coexist, and painters can switch between them.

Millet's picture angered the upper class. Here you see three poor women collecting grains on the ground. A heavy job for sore backs. In the background, we see the results of the rich landowner's harvest as a harsh contrast to the poverty and misery of these women. Such a painting was unpleasant for rich people, and it was only

after Millet's death that his art was truly recognized.

Millet belonged to the Barbizon School, a group of painters who chose to paint outdoors, known in French as *en plein air*. These artists are, to a large extent, the forerunners of those we will talk about at the end of this book: the Impressionists, the rebels who stood up against what most people considered the right way to paint. They opened the door to modern painting.

Jean-François Millet: *The Gleaners*, 1857. Musée d'Orsay, Paris

Manet
1832–1883

Edouard Manet considered himself a Realist painter, but he is often mentioned together with the Impressionists (see chapter 8) because he knew them and was a close friend to several of them. He constantly struggled to get recognition for his pictures, which annoyed him, but still, he refused to compromise. He painted the way he wanted to, and with family money supporting him, he could live comfortably, even when his paintings didn't sell.

Manet's large painting *Olympia* was exhibited at the Salon in 1865. It is strange that a picture like this should arouse so much outrage, that people should be so shocked. The critics hated the painting, saying that it was indecent, portraying a prostitute, but if we look carefully, we may recognize Titian's picture of the *Venus of Urbino* painted three hundred years earlier (see page 60-61). Manet has deliberately changed some details. Instead of a dog sleeping at her feet, there is a black cat with staring eyes. Cats in the art are often symbolic of something evil or wrong.

People turned away in disgust from this painting, and Manet was hurt by the reaction and even left the country for a while. This reaction to Manet's artwork shows us how artists of all times have been at the mercy of the general opinion around art. Just think of the "naughty" pictures painted one hundred years earlier.

And what about the maid? Why has Manet painted her black-skinned, which was unusual in France in the nineteenth century? Is it a hint to the debate around slavery that divided the United States and its civil war at the same time? Was this political hint too much for the establishment to swallow?

Now also notice the bow this woman has around her neck. Perhaps Manet wanted to ask the question: Who is truly the slave in this painting?

In *Luncheon on the Grass*, Manet also dared to challenge the contemporary view of women, and the Salon refused

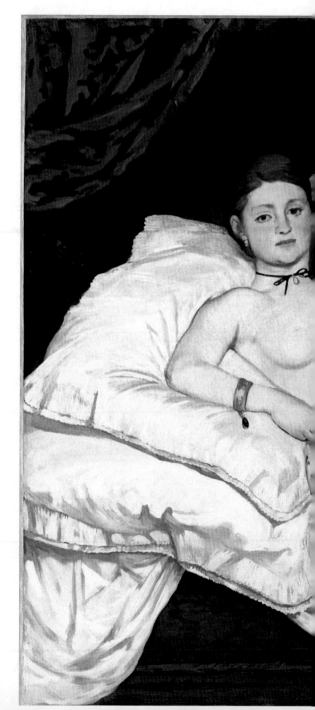

to display this picture. Critics claimed that his painting style was sloppy and the subject was highly inappropriate. Two well-dressed men are on a picnic with two women, one scantily dressed and the second nude, staring straight at us. After the rejection, Manet exhibited it at the newly established *Salon des refusés*, or the exhibition for the rejected paintings.

Manet struggled, even despaired, but his work served to inspire the young painters who appeared in Paris at this time: the Impressionists.

Edouard Manet: *Olympia*, 1863. Musée d'Orsay, Paris

Edouard Manet: *Luncheon on the Grass*, 1862-1863. Musée d'Orsay, Paris

CHAPTER 8

Impressionism

Imagine if we could travel back to Paris at the end of the nineteenth century. To be a fly on the wall in the many cafés and bars. To listen to the conversations and see the new art being created!

Paris was considered the capital of creative people, and artists flocked there from all over the world. There were painters, sculptors, photographers, writers, fashion designers, and also filmmakers. Paris brimmed with optimism, and beautiful avenues, squares, and parks were created all over the city. Paris was the place to be. And this is where Impressionism was born.

As we know, art had already been changing for decades, but with the Impressionists, there was, for the first time since the Renaissance, an absolute break with tradition. A group of painters in Paris, led by Claude Monet, were tired of spending their days in the studio with canvases that took weeks, and sometimes

Paris - A capital for creative people

months, to complete. They wanted out, literally. They wanted to paint the world as they saw it, paint the colors that changed with the light due to the time of day, the weather, and the seasons.

Photography had recently been invented and is likely part of the reason these painters began to do something completely different.

The word Impressionism is just that: impressions of reality. Moments and experiences of the here and now. Because of this sense of immediacy, the impressionists painted quickly, with big brushstrokes. Art was about capturing the moment before the moment was gone.

Another invention available at this time was *paint on tubes*. Earlier, artists had to mix their own paints, which was both difficult and time-consuming. The new practical tubes made it possible to be "on the go," and because of that, Impressionist pictures show us landscapes and gardens, but also city streets and cafés. They show life as it is at the moment of painting.

Monet
1840–1926

Claude Monet was already an accomplished painter when, in 1859, he came to Paris from Normandy to attend art school. Though he loved being in the big city, he did not feel at home in the school's studio. He wanted to go out into nature, into the light. With Renoir, Bazille, and several others, he made an extreme choice: He moved the painting outside, literally.

In this painting, we see his wife Camille and their son Jean. It is painted quickly; we can see the brush strokes in the clouds and only glimpse the faces. Such images were criticized, even ridiculed. "It's unfinished!" the critics said. "Just a rough sketch." A child must have painted it, others thought.

They did not understand that they must not observe such a picture too closely. If we stick our nose up close, we see nothing but random spots of paint. But if we step back and look at the picture from a distance, we notice the painting is more realistic than the photographically correct pictures we have seen before.

How is this possible? Let's do an experiment: Let your gaze move quickly around you. You will probably see a jumble of colors, light, and shadow. Only when you keep your head completely calm and focus on something do you see it razor-sharp. Another experiment: If you go for a quick walk in the forest or in the park, you don't see every leaf in the surrounding trees. On the other hand, you see a diffuse cloud of green. Only when you stop and focus will you see the leaves sharply. And if you talk to somebody who has the sun at her back, like Camille in this picture, you won't see her face. Not

Claude Monet: *Woman with Parasol - Madame Monet and Her Son*, 1875. National Gallery of Art, Washington D.C.

until you go close and shade your eyes from the sun will her face come into focus.

The image is an impression. A fraction of a moment. And these are the kinds of experiences we have of reality all day long.

Many years would pass before art critics and connoisseurs accepted this style of painting. The Impressionists were not allowed to exhibit their pictures at the official Salon, so they created their own exhibitions. Fortunately, Monet lived long enough for his pictures to be accepted by the Salon, and he remained faithful to Impressionism until the end of his life. Eventually, he earned enough to buy his dream house in Giverny, north of Paris, and his favorite subject was the water lilies in the garden pond.

Claude Monet:
The Japanese Bridge. Musée d'Orsay, Paris

Renoir
1841–1919

Pierre-Auguste Renoir was one of Monet's best friends and colleagues. While Monet was particularly interested in nature, Renoir mostly painted people, especially women.

He came from a working-class background and struggled financially for many years before his pictures began to sell. He is known for the following quote:

"To my mind, a picture should be something pleasant, cheerful, and pretty, yes, pretty!"

> *"To my mind, a picture should be something pleasant, cheerful, and pretty, yes pretty!"*
>
> —Pierre-Auguste Renoir

In his pictures, we see light and colors, the lightness and joy of Impressionism. But if we look extra closely, we also find the spectrum of human emotions. Renoir was clearly a connoisseur of people and above all, a good observer.

In the painting *Bal du Moulin de la Galette*, we witness an outdoor party in Montmartre in Paris. The party is well underway when we arrive, along with Renoir. And see how, with quick brushstrokes, he has painted the colors and the light of this summer scene but also captured the mood. It is as if we hear accordion music, clinking glasses, talking, and laughter. We see how sunlight filters through the trees and creates bright spots on the dark coat in the foreground. There

is *joie de vivre* (*love of life* in English), and the atmosphere is bright and comfortable. But the picture also contains drama and an array of human emotions. Do you see the young man on the far right? He stares admiringly at the woman in the middle of the picture, but she only has eyes for the man sitting with his back towards us.

Do you see the young girl leaning against the tree? Maybe she was waiting for someone; maybe she was stood up. A man tries to catch her attention, but she ignores him. And at the very back of the picture, a couple is sitting on a bench. Do you see them? They are drawn only with a few spots of blue, black, and white, but we are clearly witnessing an argument. The woman in blue wants to leave the party. The man with the top hat persuades her to stay, but I guess he has said or done something he shouldn't.

The painting is filled with such small scenes, and it is all painted quickly, before the light changes and before the colors change.

Pierre-Auguste Renoir: *Bal du Moulin de la Galette*, 1874. Musée d'Orsay, Paris

Berthe Morisot
1841–1895

Art history has mostly been written by men, about men. I am convinced there were as many creative girls as boys throughout the history of art, but they rarely had the chance to develop their talent. There are exceptions, and as mentioned in the chapter on the Baroque period (page 72) we can also assume that there are many women hidden behind artwork for which men have been given credit.

Until around 1900, the main art school in Paris, École des Beaux-Arts, was closed to women. It was considered unnatural to be independent, and even after women began to work as teachers, factory workers, and shop assistants, it was considered inappropriate for women to be professional artists.

Berthe Morisot was not only one of the first to defy the common view of women artists, but she was also one of the very first Impressionists—those rebels who defied society's view of art.

Berthe Morisot refused to let society's norms rule her, and not only did she join the Impressionists and work full-time as a painter, but she continued to do this even after she married and had children. At the time, this was completely unheard of. However, we must remember that social norms were different then, and there was still a limit as to what she could do. Berthe could not wander freely with an easel and painting supplies as her male colleagues did. Nor could she meet the others in the cafés of Montmartre, where they would sit late into the night discussing life, art, and politics.

Because of this, her art is mainly about women and children and domestic scenes, but Morisot also painted outdoor scenes in gardens and parks.

Berthe Morisot: *The Cradle*, 1872.
Musée d'Orsay, Paris

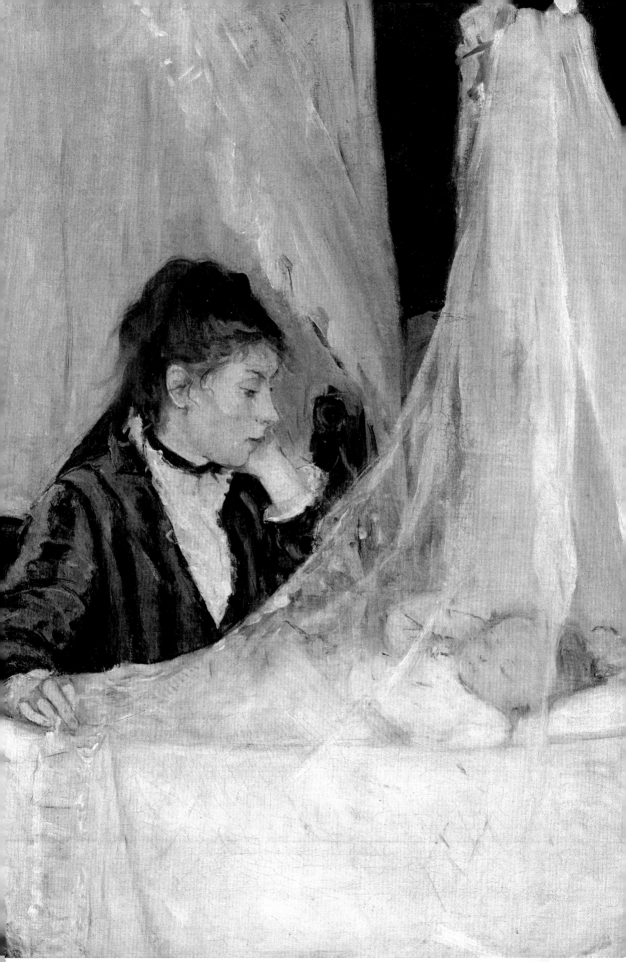

Mary Cassatt
1844–1926

Mary Cassatt was American and received an art education in Philadelphia, where they welcomed female students. However, she lived most of her adult life in France, where she became part of the Impressionist movement. She never married and never had children of her own; nevertheless, her main theme is the relationship between mother and child. In her paintings, we see a clear link to art history's greatest theme: Madonna and Child. Cassatt's models were women she knew, but in her paintings, they become timeless. These are images we can all relate to: Not everybody is a parent, but we have all been children, and we are all the son or daughter of someone, whether we know our parents or not.

Cassatt is widely credited with bringing Impressionism to the United States. She inspired other female artists because she dared to be an artist and paint differently from the norm.

Mary Cassatt: *A Goodnight Hug*, 1880. Privately owned

Mary Cassatt: *Young Mother Sewing*, 1900.
Metropolitan Museum of Art, New York

Van Gogh
1853–1870

Vincent Van Gogh was Dutch and came to Paris in the late 1880s. His dream was to live as an artist, and Paris was the place to be. He met the Impressionists and was greatly inspired by the light and colors in their paintings.

However, he had a hard time fitting in, remaining an outsider, and after a short time, he traveled south to Provence. In sunny Arles, he found what would become his style, that is, pictures filled with sunshine, vibrant colors, and powerful and decisive brushstrokes, which gave a distinctive flavor to his work.

But the world was not ready for his art. Even when Impressionism began to gain ground, Van Gogh's pictures were so different that nobody wanted to buy them. He also struggled with mental illness and spent a year in a psychiatric hospital in southern France. During that time, he painted some of his most iconic pictures. After this hospital stay, he moved back to Paris to be close to his brother but died shortly after arriving. It is unclear whether his death was a suicide.

Apart from the two paintings bought by his brother, he did not sell a single picture in his lifetime. Yet today he is considered one of the greatest artists in the Netherlands, second only to Rembrandt.

The composition, *Starry Night Over the Rhône*, was painted by a man in pain. He painted this while struggling with dark thoughts and feelings of hopelessness. The night is dark. We can barely see the houses, the boats, and the two figures in the foreground. But the stars are shining, and there are reflections of light in the river. Perhaps he, amid all that pain, knew that we need the night to see the stars, and we need darkness to be able to see the light in our own lives.

Vincent van Gogh: *Starry Night Over the Rhône*, 1888. Musée d'Orsay, Paris

Vincent van Gogh: Self Portrait, 1889. Musée d'Orsay, Paris

CHAPTER 9

Art for All Times

Western European art history does not end with Impressionism, far from it. Monet and his friends were door-openers for what we collectively call modern art. From this point on, artists went their own ways, choosing from even more styles and directions. Since then, painters and sculptors have been able to choose their path.

A few styles that emerged after Impressionism:

- Expressionism, which expresses human emotions, for example, *The Scream* by Edvard Munch.
- Cubism, which breaks up the image into pieces and puts it back together in new ways, for instance, in many of Picasso's pictures.
- Dadaism, arose as a rebellion against modern society (and the First World War) and focused on the irrational and silly. An example here is Duchamp, who exhibited an ordinary urinal and called it *Fountain*.
- Surrealism, which is about showing the absurd and dreamlike, for instance, Salvador Dalí's pictures and sculptures.

Many more "isms" have come and gone, and little by little, what we call abstract art emerged, where what we see is no longer a given, and where art is all about color and shape. I will also mention Performance Art, where the artwork becomes a performance, something that happens at the moment, and where the spectator may be invited to participate.

Finally, we have *contemporary art*, which is art created close to our own time, regardless of style.

* * *

There is so much more to be said, and this book doesn't have room for all of it. But I'll keep writing, so stay tuned!

It is worth noting that despite all the different directions and styles, the legacy

Edvard Munch: "The Scream", 1910. The Munch Museum, Oslo.

of the Renaissance lives on. We see it through how artists work and how the old motifs are still used. The artists of today stand on the shoulders of the old giants, whether they realize it or not.

How lucky we are, living today, having contemporary art at our fingertips, but also this entire legacy available—from Impressionism to the Baroque, the Renaissance, and everything in between.

By the way, remember what we talked about at the beginning of this book. Art speaks a language that is not aimed primarily at our intellect. It gives us a language to deal with what we have no language for. And we can all find works of art that speak to us exactly where we are in life. Art that challenges or delights us, provokes or comforts us.

You may see works of art that remind you that you are human. That you, deep down, remain that curious child who finds the world exciting and always discovers something new to learn.

Also, don't forget what I said in the first chapter: You are more than good enough when it comes to experiencing art. Your experiences and your life story make the experience personal for just you.

Don't be afraid of what you don't know about art; instead, allow wonder to take place, and keep asking questions!

When you see works of art, also try to let the painting or sculpture speak to you. Suddenly, you may find answers that you didn't even know you already had within you.

As you grow more eager to learn and enjoy art, I hope you remember the Restaurant Method. Choose only a few works of art or a few rooms in the museum. Our minds cannot handle too much information at a time—you are allowed to pick some and leave out the rest.

We have traveled long and far now, from antiquity to the present day, from Florence to Oslo. I'm so glad you joined me on this discovery trip, and who knows, maybe one day we'll embark on a new journey together.

Sources

Aubert, Karl Egil: *Det gylne snit*, from: *Store norske leksikon* (www.snl.no)

Knut Berg/Norsk malerkunst 1993 ISBN 82-05-20587-6

Illustrations

These are either my own, or they are in the open, without copyright, mostly found through Wikimedia Commons or the web pages of Museums. In a few cases I have the name of the photographer, but in many cases (Wikimedia) I haven't been able to find it.

Kristine T. G. Hardeberg: (Chapter 2 and 4)

Wikimedia Commons

Wikimedia / G CHP (Versailles, chapter 5)

National Museum of Oslo

National Museum of Oslo/ Børre Høstland (Kittelsen, Chapter 1)

Lascaux IV (https://www.lascaux.fr) (Cave paintings, chapter 2)

The Vatican Museums: Museo Chiaramonti (Augustus, Chapter 3)

Museo dell'Opera Metropolitana del Duomo (Duccio, Chapter 3))

Joaquim Alves Gaspar / Wikimedia (Saint Peter's Church, Chapter 4)

About the Author

Kristine T. G. Hardeberg is a Norwegian author, speaker, and art history influencer. For more than a decade, she has helped thousands of people from all around the world discover how fun and exciting art history is. She has lived for years in the US and France and spends a lot of time in Italy, but her main home is in Norway. Kristine is married to Jon, and they have four children, one grandchild, and two cats.

Connect at KristineTGHardeberg.no.

DO YOU WANT TO LEARN MORE WITH KRISTINE?

Kristine has prepared a fun mini-lecture for you. Sign up for her newsletter - and watch it when convenient for you.

CONNECT WITH KRISTINE

Follow her on your favorite social media platforms today.

kristinetghardeberg.no

THIS BOOK IS PROTECTED INTELLECTUAL PROPERTY

The author of this book values Intellectual Property. The book you just read is protected by Easy IP™, a proprietary process, which integrates blockchain technology giving Intellectual Property "Global Protection." By creating a "Time-Stamped" smart contract that can never be tampered with or changed, we establish "First Use" that tracks back to the author.

Easy IP™ functions much like a Pre-Patent™ since it provides an immutable "First Use" of the Intellectual Property. This is achieved through our proprietary process of leveraging blockchain technology and smart contracts. As a result, proving "First Use" is simple through a global and verifiable smart contract. By protecting intellectual property with blockchain technology and smart contracts, we establish a "First to File" event.

Powered By Easy IP™

LEARN MORE AT EASYIP.TODAY

Made in United States
North Haven, CT
31 October 2023

43425663R00073